When words
matter most

When words

Thoughtful Words and Deeds to Express Just the Right Thing at Just the Right Time

matter most

Robyn Freedman Spizman

CROWN PUBLISHERS, INC.

NEW YORK

Published by Crown Publishers, Inc.,
201 East 50th Street, New York, New York 10022.
Member of the Crown Publishing Group.

Random House, Inc. New York, Toronto, London, Sydney, Auckland
http://www.randomhouse.com/

CROWN and colophon are trademarks of Crown Publishers, Inc.

Printed in the United States of America

Design by Nancy Kenmore
Illustrations by Fausta Tamburino

Library of Congress Cataloging-in-Publication Data
is available upon request.

ISBN 0-517-70406-4

10 9 8 7 6 5

To my wonderful family...
who are never at a loss for words.
I love you—Robyn.

Contents

Foreword

Ever since I can remember, I've had a love affair with words. As a little girl I wrote poems for my family members and teachers. Never at a loss for words, I loved expressing myself in creative ways. As an adult, however, I've discovered that people are often surprised by my endless words of praise. My experiences reinforce the fact that too few of us acknowledge our true feelings and express what we think.

I wrote this book because of a simple premise that I believe in my heart—that words really matter. As we meet daily challenges, the words we use have a lasting effect on our lives and the lives of those around us. Words are the messages we use to keep us believing in ourselves and validate who we are. The art of giving a compliment or expressing a feeling is a precious skill that everyone can acquire. Receiving praise is also an art, as we learn to accept positive thoughts that others bestow on us.

When Words Matter Most is a book that I hope will make a difference in your life because it celebrates the art of self-expression. It offers caring gestures and meaningful words to use for all occasions. For those of us who grew up hearing positive words, relating our feelings comes easy. Many of us, however, struggle with expressing ourselves; we worry that we might look foolish and often don't know what to say at certain times.

If this book inspires you to do one thing, I hope it will help you connect with the positive feelings you have for yourself and for others and express them. I hope you will let go of any hesitation, procrastination, and trepidation and say what you feel! Focus on the smallest kindness another person extends to you and compliment it;

then watch the good that grows as a result of your positive reinforcement.

Life is a montage of memorable moments. And when all is said and done, it's often the words, the conversations, the letters, the cards, the small deeds that we do which we hold dear as time passes. Words are the tools we use to stay connected with each other always. By offering words that help you to soothe a soul, celebrate a life, or recognize another person, this book will help you enrich life's most meaningful moments.

It is my hope that this collection of thoughts, ideas, and actions will help you spread compassion and thoughtfulness in your corner of the world. Consider the words in this book as inspiration for celebrating yourself, the people you encounter in your everyday life, and those who mean the most to you. Let others know your feelings. Express your appreciation and inner thoughts every chance you get, and let this book guide you down the rich path of sharing with the people around you.

Words are the medium with which the soul paints a picture. Challenge yourself and others to paint masterpieces. Make your journey in life full of memories and free of regrets. As you paint a picture of your experiences, let words be the colors you use to enliven your spirit and guide your soul.

And remember that words are free, recyclable, politically and environmentally correct, natural, and fat-free, and their proper use can encourage, inspire, motivate, activate, and, on top of it all, perpetuate and personify goodness. When you think that your words will make a difference, use them. They are yours for the giving.

When words
matter most

1

Choosing Words for Every Occasion

I expect to pass through life but once. If there-
fore, there be any kindness I can show, or any
good thing I can do to any fellow being, let me do
it now, and not defer or neglect it, as I shall not
pass this way again.

—WILLIAM PENN

As we pass through this life, each of us has an opportunity to identify meaningful moments with our unique signature. We use words as tools to accomplish this. Our word choices are endless and offer great potential for us to embellish every occasion. No matter where we go or what we do daily, the words we use help us connect in large and small ways with each other.

Can you think of an occasion when you wanted to say just the right thing at the right time, or send a note or special words that would help or encourage someone during a difficult time? At one point or another, we have all discovered the power of carefully chosen words.

Perhaps you are someone who seizes every moment and occasion and already values expressing your feelings and compassion for others. Or you may be someone who wants to use positive or meaningful words more often. As you spread a thought, express your feelings of appreciation, and offer words of concern, you'll discover one of the greatest opportunities in life—to make someone else feel special.

When you praise others, it then becomes their choice whether or not to accept those pearls of kindness and use them to their full potential. As you use words to augment every occasion, consider new and creative ways to express yourself and make a difference in others' lives. By recognizing an occasion in some unique and special way, you truly identify your special signature in life, one that will always be remembered and ultimately matter most to all around you.

Choose Your Words Wisely

The art of being wise is the art of knowing what to overlook.

—WILLIAM JAMES

We all have the chance to choose words that help or words that hurt. So what makes one person positive and the next negative? What allows one person to see a glass half full and another half empty? We all come from different experiences in life, but being positive or negative is ultimately your choice.

For those of us who are positive and draw on inspiring thoughts to move through life's challenges, words and acts of kindness become our fuel, our invaluable source of energy. Choosing words wisely enables us to use them to their fullest potential. The one thing most people who are at ease with self-expression have in common is that they speak from their heart. That doesn't come easy for everyone. In fact, for many it's quite difficult. So stop before you speak. And when in doubt, remember that less is more: there are times when giving someone a hug, an "I care about you," or an "I'm thinking of you" is enough.

Words to Inspire Yourself

Change your thoughts and you change your world.

—NORMAN VINCENT PEALE

Our life is a summation of our words, our deeds, and our thoughts. Each of us has daily conversations that affect our actions. We also have endless opportunities to follow through with deeds that we feel good about.

How often do you find yourself saying phrases like "I need to call so and so" or "I need to write a note of thanks." Or even "I need to tell my family I love them." Individuals in touch with their feelings often check up on themselves with "word wake-ups"—those little internal prompters that gently remind us to think of others. One trick I have learned over time is to ask myself, "Whom do I need to thank lately? Whom do I need to check up on? Who needs to hear from me? Who has done something of value that matters to me?"

These questions that I ask myself keep me in touch with what matters to me: thinking of others. We can all be our own cheerleader urging us back into the ring one more time, to keep plugging away even when it's tough, to face the difficulties in life, to say "I'm sorry."

It's easy to become so overwhelmed in life that we turn to negative thoughts that become habitual obstacles. We often forget all the wonderful things that we do and instead focus on details that are destructive. Getting in touch with the good we do helps put life in perspective when it gets too crazy.

While we don't always have time to spend being thoughtful, doing acts of kindness often just takes minutes. A telephone call, a greeting card, a condolence note, a poem—whatever you can manage will take just a moment of your time. Thinking a thank-you doesn't get it there. Feeling love doesn't equal giving someone a hug or telling them you love them. Consider what new thoughts you can say to yourself that will help you reach the road of generosity and compassion.

Actions Speak as Loud as Words

Action is eloquence.
—WILLIAM SHAKESPEARE

We've all heard the old cliché "Actions speak louder than words." Well, thoughts put into actions are exactly what this book is about. Actions and words speak equally as loud when they express one's innermost thoughts. Actions are simply words set free and put into motion.

Words matter most when you follow through with a promise, a commitment. Words are meaningless when they are insincere and empty of promise and lack the action that makes them believable. There is no replacement for sincerity. Words are the medium, the matter that adds substance to the thought. Putting them into action brings them alive and offers you rewarding experiences.

As you read and use this book, I've suggested many ways to recognize every occasion in life, to offer you a source to turn to as you find ways to add your own creative adaptations. From times of joy to times of sorrow, from times of happiness to times of despair, choose your words wisely and honor their presence in your life. Words are truly a gift you can give that will add meaning to your life and to others along the way.

Words That Last a Lifetime

Every man is a quotation from all his ancestry.

—RALPH WALDO EMERSON

Every word, quote, or inspiration we write, hear, or speak has an origin deeply rooted in the spirit of mankind throughout history. The words might change, but the thoughts and sentiments remain the same.

An old Japanese proverb says, "One kind word can warm three winter months." Words have always been a powerful and meaningful means for connecting us with each other as we use them in tribute to one another's deeds and actions. The words in this book are based on a simple premise—that our words can last a lifetime if we take the time to value their importance.

As I have reviewed many letters of historical significance, it amazes me how valuable others' words have remained over the years. The following selections were used to close correspondence by some well-known individuals. Each person chose to end his or her letters with words of affection, sincerity, and kindness. As you begin your journey with words, consider creating a few salutations that become your signature expressions. Consider your closing as important as your opening and make every word count.

As the first signer of the Declaration of Independence, John Hancock immortalized himself and left his mark on time just by his signature. Here's your opportunity to leave yours!

How the Famous Sign Off

Yours affectionately, John Q. Adams (a letter, 1803).

Your much obliged friend, James Buchanan (a letter, 1867).

Respectfully, A. Lincoln (a letter, 1863).

I have the honour with great respects & c. David Crockett (a letter, 1830).

If I may be of service to you at any time, please be sure to write me. You have my very best wishes for success and I am, Cordially yours, Wyatt S. Earp (a letter, 1928).

Faithfully yours, T. Roosevelt (a letter, 1919).

With best wishes, Amelia Earhart.

In cordial devotion, and with many regards to your wife. freud. (a letter from Sigmund Freud, 1920).

Yrs. sincerely, A. Graham Bell (a letter, 1873).

Sincerely Yours, Albert Einstein (an autographed photograph, 1933).

In appreciation & with sincere good wishes, George Gershwin (a signed copy of his songbook, 1932).

Always your affectionate, Dad (a letter from Frank L. Baum to his son, 1910).

Truly Yours, Mark Twain (autographed postcard, 1902).

2

Words of Encouragement and Praise

Think . . . of the world you carry within you.
—RAINER MARIA RILKE

This chapter presents words of encouragement and praise—those words that inspire us and motivate us in life. Encouragement is one of the most important things we can give each other. The following quotes, words, and ideas for encouraging others are yours for the choosing. Encouragement is a lasting gift which helps us be the best we can be. It's up to us to find meaningful ways to use it often.

Words of encouragement are also always appropriate. Whether someone wins or loses a game, words of inspiration and praise matter. They don't always solve a problem, but they can make a difference and help a loved one feel better. Whether someone is feeling blue, has had a setback in life, or just needs a pat on the back, encouraging words will uplift.

Encouragement also comes in many forms. The following examples offer you a variety of choices of words and creative ideas for encouraging and motivating others. Search for new ways to use them and celebrate their importance in your life.

Quotes of Encouragement

One's destination is never a place but rather a new way of looking at things.

—HENRY MILLER

Good, better best,
Never rest,
Till good be better and better best.

—MOTHER GOOSE

Don't say: Someday I'll begin
When my lucky ship comes in.
You must launch your ship to win;
Right now is the answer then.

—ADAPTATION OF A QUOTE BY
FERDINAND VOLLENDER

The word impossible was a mistake. It's really I'm Possible!

—AUTHOR

Whatever is worth doing at all is worth doing well.

—LORD CHESTERFIELD

Love the moment and the energy of that moment will spread beyond all boundaries.

—CORITA KENT

There is no security on this earth. There is only opportunity.

—DOUGLAS MACARTHUR

I long to accomplish a great and noble task but it is my chief duty to accomplish small tasks as if they were great and noble.

—HELEN KELLER

The true perfection of man lies not in what man has, but in what man is.

—OSCAR WILDE

Life is the gift of nature; but beautiful living is the gift of wisdom.

—GREEK ADAGE

Remember, no one can make you feel inferior without your consent.

—ELEANOR ROOSEVELT

Do what you can, with what you have, where you are.

—THEODORE ROOSEVELT

He who has conquered doubt and fear has conquered failure.

—JAMES LANE ALLEN

It may be those who do most, dream most.

—STEPHEN LEACOCK

Man is what he believes.

—ANTON CHEKHOV

Courage is grace under pressure.

—ERNEST HEMINGWAY

Hitch your wagon to a star; Keep your seat and there you are.

—ANONYMOUS

Often the test of courage is not to die but to live.

—CONTE VITTORIO ALFIERI

Some people may have greatness thrust upon them. Very few have excellence thrust upon them.

—JOHN GARDNER

There is no medicine like hope, no incentive so great, and no tonic so powerful as expectation of something tomorrow.

—ORISON S. MARDEN

Life does not have to be easy to be wonderful.

—ANONYMOUS

Without knowing the force of words, it is impossible to know men.

—CONFUCIUS

It is easy to flatter; it is harder to praise.

—JEAN PAUL RICHTER

Focus on making things better, not bigger.

—H. JACKSON BROWN, JR.

An aim in life is the only fortune worth finding. And it is not to be found in foreign lands, but in the heart itself.

—ROBERT LOUIS STEVENSON

It's what you learn after you know it all that counts.

—JOHN WOODEN

A diamond is a chunk of coal that did good under pressure.

—MOUNTAIN SAYING

The wise don't expect to find life worth living; they make it that way.

—COOKIE CUNNINGHAM

Not knowing when the dawn will come, / I open every door.

—EMILY DICKINSON

We can do anything we want to if we stick to it long enough.

—HELEN KELLER

Other Words of Encouragement

GREAT stands for: Get Ready for Everything And Try.

The opposite of "no" is "on"!

A good character carries with it the highest power of causing a thing to be believed.

YOU stands for: Your Opportunity is Unlimited!

Have I told you how great you are lately?

Be your best. Be yourself.

You never cease to amaze me.

You have set such a wonderful example for others.

You never give up. I notice how hard you try.

If it's to be, it's up to me.

A STORY OF ENCOURAGEMENT. Try writing a story or making an analogy. Here's one that I received from a special friend named Deborah, after helping her with a charitable cause. I read it often for encouragement and treasure it beyond words.

THE TUGBOAT

In a stormy sea of doubt, I push through the waters guided by a dream. I have a personal tugboat in my life; she guides me gently through the proper rivers of learning—tugging, pulling, but never shoving. Human awareness dominates her life. She is the shining light onto everything she encounters.

You know within minutes of the first encounter that she has guided several ships through rough water, and learned from each experience. It would not have been possible for me to get to my dream port without her, had she not been steadfast with me, if not in person, in spirit.

It will be difficult to convey my appreciation totally. I offer my friendship and loyalty, two things I value highly, for I offer that to only a few who I know can appreciate the gift.

This ship may be small, but she has the ability to maneuver all the big lumbering boats onto the direct route to success. I hope that when I venture out to sea, and into a new direction, she will be there—always dependable, always giving of herself and daring to venture in the dark seas with you. To say that she is a friend is what I consider my good fortune.

DEBORAH REEVES-BRANNON

Acts of Encouragement

STICK WITH ME. Place self-sticking notes in special places where they will be found at unexpected times. Write statements like "I'll stick by your side no matter what" or "I'm proud of you . . . keep sticking to it!"

BE THERE AND CHEER LOUD. There's nothing as great as hearing someone who cares about you yell your name or clap for you at an event!

NOTE THIS. Tuck a note in a child's lunch box. Include a note on an apple that says, "You're the apple of my eye!"

JUST NOTICE. Acknowledge someone who is doing a terrific job. Let them know that you notice what a great effort they are making. Say it, fax it, write it, sing it—just do it!

BECOME A SECRET ADMIRER. Put a card in the mailbox of someone who needs an encouraging word. Sign it from a secret admirer who thinks they are great!

GET SMART. Ask someone you care about who has inspired or encouraged them most in life. Learn from their answers. You'll be surprised how much you'll find out about encouragement.

SMART COOKIES. Send someone a box or arrangement of cookies with a note that says, "You're the smartest cookie I know."

AND THE WINNER IS . . . Give someone you want to encourage their name in an envelope like one from the Emmy Awards and tell them they're a winner!

A PENNY FOR YOUR THOUGHTS. Go to the bank and get a bunch of shiny new pennies. Give them out to "shining examples" of people you appreciate. Tell them they shine in your book!

STEP RIGHT UP. Choose a leader or role model who has bettered our world and reminds you of a special person in your life. Give your friend a book all about that famous individual, and tell them they follow in the person's footsteps!

THEY'LL GET A KICK OUT OF THIS. Arrange to borrow a pair of your friend's shoes. Have them gift wrapped and give them to your friend with a note that reads, "No one could fill your shoes."

GO TO GREAT LENGTHS TO ENCOURAGE SOMEONE. With a marker pen on a roll of calculator paper, write one of the following over and over to make a super long message:

> I'd go to any lengths to encourage you!
> You're on a roll . . . go for it!
> I'm cheering you on and on and on and on!

IT'S NEVER TOO LATE. Think of someone—a friend, family member, or teacher—who played an important role in your life and helped you to be the person you are today. Write them a letter of encouragement and praise them. Return the kindness they once showed you; you'll be glad you did.

ART FROM THE HEART. Frame your child's artwork and display it in a special place in your home. As the years go by, it will become one of your most precious possessions. It also tells your child how much their efforts and ideas matter to you.

ENCOURAGEMENT AWARD. Give an award to someone who encourages you. Have a plaque made in their honor or present them a loving cup for being so caring.

THEY'LL EAT IT UP. When someone you know is having a tough time, call them a day ahead and tell them a surprise meal will be arriving. Prepare something special and attach a clever note to your edible gift. For example, bring pasta and add a note that reads, "The pastabilities are limitless!" Or send a deli sandwich piled high with a note that says, "You'll always be my hero!"

LEAVE THEM FEELING BETTER. Attach a note to a beautiful fall leaf you find on the ground, with the words "I'll always be-leave in you!"

RELAX . . . SEND A FAX. Send a VIP fax to a Very Inspiring, Impressive, Important Person in your life. Name all the fax/facts about them that come to mind. For example: "Fax About Willy . . . He's kind, loving, wonderful, and always on my mind!"

SEALED WITH A KISS. Send someone a box filled with Hershey Kisses with a card that reads, "All the kisses in the world aren't enough for you!" or "When you need a kiss and I'm not there, try one of these and know I care!"

DAILY ENCOURAGEMENT. Wrap up a calendar for someone you want to encourage with a note that reads, "I believe in you every day of the year!"

CREATE A FAN CLUB. Give someone special a small desk-sized fan with a card that says, "Love from your greatest fan!"

FOOD FOR THOUGHT. Put a note in the refrigerator or on a family member's favorite food, one they're bound to see, with a note that says, "Food for thought—you're terrific!"

AT THE SOUND OF THE BEEP. Leave an encouraging voice message on someone's answering machine that says something very positive about them that you appreciate. At the end of the message, tell them to replay this five times, because hearing it once won't do it justice.

SWEET DREAMS. Place a note under your child's or a family member's pillow. Whether they lost a game or had a rough day, a few encouraging words will help. Write something special like "Sweet dreams to the sweetest kid in the world."

CALL 1-800-SEND-A-SONG. Send-A-Song for approximately $9.95. Choose from hundreds of songs, including "What a Wonderful World," "Lean on Me," "You're the Top," "Climb Every Mountain," or "[The Sun Will Come Up] Tomorrow." This musical telegram also lets you personalize your song with a twenty-second prerecorded message, and it can be sent any time and day you specify. Send-A-Song will definitely give anyone's day a lift!

MAKE HEADLINES. When you read in the newspaper about someone's particular accomplishment, send a note with the clipping that says you noticed!

THINGS WILL BRIGHTEN UP SOON. Send a pair of inexpensive sunglasses or a light bulb with a note attached that says, "Things will brighten up soon!"

ALL WOUND UP? Send a windup toy to someone who's stressed out and needs some encouragement. Add a note that says, "In case you get too wound up, wind this up instead!"

DO NOT PASS GO. Give the game of Monopoly with these words attached: "To our favorite player . . . we're banking on you!"

WHEN LIFE'S A "BEACH." Send an inflatable beachball with a note that says, "We know you will bounce back soon!"

3

Words of Joy

To be able to find joy in another's joy; that is the
secret of happiness.

—GEORGES BERNANOS

Words of joy celebrate another individual's happiness as if it were
your own. These words seem to come easily, but summing up the
happiest moments requires creativity and a sincere desire to share another's good fortune and to speak from the heart. The real secret of
happiness is concentrating on the goodness in others.

This chapter presents creative ways to join in others' happiness,
celebrate someone's birthday, and acknowledge other special times.
Happiness, though, doesn't always have to be centered around an occasion. Some of my favorite words of joy have been sent to me for no
special reason at all.

Quotes of Joy

Happiness

Happiness is the only good. The time to be happy is
now. The place to be happy is here. The way to be happy
is to make other people happy.

—ROBERT G. INGERSOLL

The joy of the heart gives a smile a jump start.

—AUTHOR

Happiness sneaks in through a door you didn't know you left open.

—JOHN BARRYMORE

Those who bring sunshine to the lives of others cannot keep it from themselves.

—JAMES M. BARRIE

Happiness is someone to love, something to do, and something to hope for.

—OLD CHINESE PROVERB

It is not in doing what you like, but in liking what you do that is the secret of happiness.

—JAMES M. BARRIE

Birthdays

Age is the acceptance of a term of years. But maturity is the glory of years.

—MARTHA GRAHAM

Age is a question of mind over matter. If you don't mind, it doesn't matter!

—FOLK PROVERB

You are never too old to become younger.

—MAE WEST

We are always the same age inside.

—GERTRUDE STEIN

As long as one can admire and love, one is young forever.

—PABLO CASALS

The wiser mind mourns less for what age takes away,
than what it leaves behind.

—WILLIAM WORDSWORTH

A diplomat is a man who never forgets a lady's birthday,
but never remembers her age.

—ANONYMOUS

The first hundred years are the toughest.

—BELLE BROWN

At fifty, everyone has the face he deserves.

—GEORGE ORWELL

Forty is the old age of youth; fifty is the youth of old age.

—FRENCH PROVERB

Old age isn't so bad when you consider the alternative.

—MAURICE CHEVALIER

Happy Birthday

Birthdays are a special time that celebrate life. Over the years I have
learned to love every birthday as if I were a child. Being a gracious re-
ceiver of all this attention is as important as giving, so consider the
time and effort everyone extends on your behalf.

The following ideas are clever ways for making each and every
birthday special and marking the moment with a memorable gift.

Greetings from the White House!

Here's a wonderful opportunity to send the greeting of a lifetime from the President and the First Lady. For anyone eighty years old or over, you can request a birthday card from the White House. All requests are due in writing six weeks in advance. This special tradition honoring these great big birthdays has been in effect since the Eisenhower administration. Send your request in writing with the birthday girl or boy's name, address, and birth date, including the year, to The Greetings Office, Room 39, The White House, Washington, DC 20500.

A Birthday Rhyme

A birthday rhyme is always fun to receive. Try creating some of your own for size:

Birthdays come and birthdays go;
On you the years they hardly show;
We're thrilled you're (fifty), we think that's great—
Here's to (fifty) more . . . we can hardly wait!

Birthdays are a funny thing—
The same old song we always sing.
But——, when it is your turn,
We'll be watching all those candles burn!

We're big on birthdays,
This is true . . .
That's why we're celebrating
You! You! You!

Birthdays come but once a year,
And we're so happy yours is here.
So, our friend, we wish for you
That you reach a hundred and two!

———, ———, this poem's for you,
With happy wishes the whole year through.

The thoughts tucked in this little card
Hold lots of wishes, too.
They're meant for someone special,
And that someone is you!

B is for Birthday, yours is here!
I is for I'm wishing you lots of good cheer.
R is for Ready, let's have some fun.
T is for Telling everyone!
H is for Happiness, the whole year through.
D is for Did you say how old are you?
A is for Always make a wish.
Y is for You deserve all of this!

We always are in a hurry,
But today's a special day,
So I'm slowing down my speed
To wish you right of way.
I heard it is your birthday
So I'm changing gears, take heed,
To stop and say Happy Birthday . . .
May you never slow your speed!

CLEVER BIRTHDAY GIFTS

SEND A SONG. One of my favorite gifts of all time is to send a song to someone special with your own personalized prerecorded twenty-second message. Call 1-800-SEND-A-SONG and they will fax or mail you a list of songs. You can also sample and hear a few great suggestions. The price is approximately $9.95 for one song or you can purchase them as a package and save. This customized service allows you to program the time it will be sent or you can send it immediately. (It's great for those last-minute words and wishes you need to send.) Here are some of my birthday favorites.

"Thank You for Being a Friend"

"Young at Heart"

 "Happy Birthday"

"You Say It's Your Birthday"

"What a Wonderful World"

"I Just Called to Say I Love You"

This idea is also perfect for saying "I'm sorry," "Cheer up," "Get well" ("Don't Worry . . . Be Happy")—you name it!

CALLING ALL COOKIE LOVERS. Say Happy Birthday to a sharp cookie. Call 1-888-922-3535 to order the Famous 4th Street Cookie Company's fabulous award-winning cookies. For more than seventeen years in Philadelphia, this company has baked eight varieties of outrageous handmade, hand-packed cookies averaging $19.95 per dozen. This cost includes a gift box, enclosure card, and

second-day Federal Express shipping. Add a sweet message . . . Chocolate Chip: "Happy Birthday to a chip off the old block!" Peanut Butter: "You butter have a Happy Birthday!"

SEND A PIECE OF CAKE. Call 1-800-9-CAKE-90 or 404-351-CAKE (local in Atlanta) and send a delicious pound cake from A Piece of Cake. Their motto is "They Take the Cake. Anywhere!" Their cakes are delivered in bright, shiny decorator tins with a special gift card from you! They've also got fabulous candles to be included with orders only . . . candles that sparkle, won't blow out, and even song candles that'll hum a perfect rendition of "Happy Birthday." Should you want more, ask about their mean bag of coffee. The pound cake can be shipped anywhere and is approximately $32 for regular UPS delivery; two-day delivery is available for an added charge. Great notes to include: "You take the cake" or "Hope your birthday is a piece of cake!"

A SIGN OF THE TIME. Deliver that day's horoscope in a birthday card with a note that says, "All signs point to a Happy Birthday for ———."

Aquarius	January 20–February 18
Pisces	February 19–March 20
Aries	March 21–April 19
Taurus	April 20–May 20
Gemini	May 21–June 20
Cancer	June 21–July 22
Leo	July 23–August 22
Virgo	August 23–September 22
Libra	September 23–October 22
Scorpio	October 23–November 21

| Sagittarius | November 22–December 21 |
| Capricorn | December 22–January 19 |

TIE THIS ONE ON. Tie the end of a ball of yarn to a birthday gift and then unravel the yarn all over the house. What fun the birthday child will have finding it!

BIRTHDAY WAKE-UP. One of my favorite surprises on my birthday was when I turned thirteen and woke up to a beautifully wrapped box from my parents. I'll never forget how surprised I was to wake up and remember it was my special day!

GO OVERBOARD. Find out the person's favorite candy or fruit and send tons of it on their birthday! My husband sent me pounds of my favorite candy with a note that said, "I'm stuck on you!" A friend of ours had a farmer drive a truckload of strawberries to their house to surprise his wife. The note: "I'm berry in love with you!" I promise, whatever you do in quantity, they'll never forget it.

START A TRADITION. My friends and I go out together for lunch for each of our birthdays. On my birthday, I decided I would give my friends a gift for being so wonderful all year long, and I wrote each of them a poem. When it was time for dessert, I had the waiter deliver the notes on a silver platter! Everyone loved her poem and the next thing I knew they all felt compelled to do something creative on their birthdays, too. So now, at every lunch, the birthday girl gives a favor or does something special. Here's what we've done this year:

Patty brought a bag of garden vegetables to wish everyone a healthy season. Lori sang a song, right there in the restaurant! Gail brought each of us a book from a secondhand book sale. Norma filled coffee mugs with travel guides to New York, her hometown. And Ava brought the gang a goodie bag of candy—fat-free, of course.

BIRTHDAY TREASURES. One group of friends I know brings to every birthday celebration the same centerpiece, which gets recycled birthday to birthday. They use a large snow dome with a birthday theme inside. Each time it shows up, it brings back memories and it's always given to the birthday honoree who's next on the list to enjoy it until they get together again.

WRAP IT UP. My friend Lynn shared her favorite birthday gift of all time. On a particular birthday when her family and friends weren't in town, her husband, Don, wanted to make sure she was deluged with presents on her actual birthday. So he wrapped up thirty large boxes in colorful wrapping paper and when Lynn got home, the entire room was filled. Each box contained one item, ranging from magazines to candy bars to a deck of cards, and Lynn says it was the best birthday ever. Whoever said it's the thought that counts must have known Don!

TOYS TO GROW ON. Call 1-800-542-8338 for an outstanding toy catalog featuring the most creative and clever toys you'll ever find. From outrageous arts and crafts kits to perfect toys for the great pretender at your house, shop until you drop with this fabulous resource for kids. The catalog is free and you can call them twenty-four hours a day. They will wrap your gift, add a card, and ship it anywhere. When sending an art kit, have the card say, "Have lots of laughs with these arts and crafts!" Or send a game with the message "Hope your birthday is fun and games!"

PROFILES IN HISTORY. Call 1-800-942-8856 and speak to the nation's leading dealer in guaranteed authentic, original historical autographs. They buy and sell top-quality material in every field, from presidents to authors to sports heroes and Hollywood legends,

and each item comes with a lifetime guarantee of authenticity. Prices start at $100 and go up, depending on the rarity of the item. A general information brochure is available upon request, and they also offer archival framing services. Match a clever note with the gift, such as "Happy Birthday to a legend of our time" or "Happy Birthday to someone who is priceless!"

THE RIGHT START. Call 1-800-LITTLE-1. Here's a super catalog for infants, young children, and the families who love them. It has a great selection of gifts for those brand-new birthdays. Gift certificates are available.

CALLING ALL PARTY ANIMALS. Call 1-800-445-8642 and order the Animal Town catalog, a fantastic creative birthday resource filled with toys, games, and books for cooperative learning and endless fun.

I'm Happy for You

When you express happiness for someone else, you send a message straight from the heart. Think of the people you care about who are celebrating a special time in their lives. How can you let them know you are happy for them? Celebrating someone else's accomplishment, promotion, or special moment helps you to recognize that person in a meaningful way. You might do it in a letter:

> Dear——,
>   You did it again. I wanted to tell you how happy I am for you. Your accomplishment is remarkable, but then again I always knew you could do it!

WRITE A POEM IN THEIR HONOR

Happiness is all around you—
All you have to do is look,
Because of all the thoughtful deeds
And time you always took.
It rests inside a thankful heart
With words and smiles that say . . .
Happiness is all around you
For you give it every day.

Dear ——,
I am so proud of you;
You amaze us all
With all you do;
You're really terrific,
Absolutely outrageous—
Your enthusiasm for life
Is totally contagious.

I'm just elated—
Make that ecstatic,
Impressed—
With all you do!
That's really great you did it . . .
Gosh, we're proud of you!

What a Wonderful World
Because of You

Sometimes you just want to let someone special know how much they mean to you and everyone around them. Here are some ways to get that message across.

SEND A SPECIAL POEM

The world's a kinder, gentler place
Because you occupy some space.

Bravo, Hooray, Congratulations,
It's a fabulous day for a celebration.
You didn't hear? You haven't been told?
We're celebrating you and your heart of gold!

CREATIVE GIFTS FOR CELEBRATING
OTHERS AND SPREADING JOY

SEND A FLASHLIGHT. Tell someone the world's a brighter place because they are in it!

HAVE A NOVEL EXPERIENCE WITH SOMEONE. Give your favorite novel with a card that says, "It's been a novel experience knowing you."

THINK THE WORLD OF SOMEONE. Give them a map of the world tied up in a ribbon with a note that says, "I think the world of you!"

DELIVER A DICTIONARY. Give someone who is extraordinary a dictionary and underline with a highlighter all the words in it that describe that individual. From Astounding to Fabulous to Marvelous, don't miss a word! Add a note that says, "I've underlined words from A to Z, to show how much you mean to me!"

A GIFT FROM THE HOLE BUNCH. Has someone brought your family a "hole" lot of joy? Send a dozen doughnuts or doughnut holes to make your point.

HAS SOMEONE SWEETENED YOUR LIFE? Send dozens of Almond Joy candy bars to let them know they've brought joy to your life.

POPPING WITH JOY? If you're popping with joy or glad someone special popped into your life, send a tin of popcorn to let them know.

Spreading Holiday Joy

Joy is a year-round celebration, but here are some creative resources for spreading a little extra joy during the holidays.

BOOKS ARE BEST. Give a copy of *The Little Book of Christmas Joys: 432 Things to Do for Yourself and Others That Just Might Make This the Best Christmas Ever* by H. Jackson Brown, Jr., Rosemary Brown, and Kathy Peel (Rutledge Hill Press, 1994). Add a note that says, "May the joys of Christmas be yours all year long!"

ORDER THE SOURCE FOR EVERYTHING JEWISH. Call 1-800-426-2567 and request a catalog from the leading resource for Judaica gifts and products for the entire year. From gourmet goodies to great gifts, books, and toys, this is a one-stop shop.

TUNE IN ON THE HOLIDAYS. Order the Signals catalog by calling 1-800-663-9994. This is a wonderful catalog for fans and friends of public television. Filled with fabulous gifts that inform, enlighten, and entertain, it's jam-packed with gifts for the holidays and more!

A GIFT FOR ALL SEASONS. Call 1-800-756-6787 and order Seasons, a terrific gift catalog focused on special occasions. From Halloween to Valentine's Day to graduation, whenever there's a joyous event, Seasons has the perfect gift.

SEASON'S EATINGS. Say Happy Holidays to a smart cookie! Call 1-800-825-1613 weekdays and order Brent & Sam's cookie catalog. Their cookies come with a warning: *Do not* dunk Brent & Sam's cookies in coffee, tea, or milk. They become *totally* irresistible. I found out the hard way!

START A HOLIDAY TRADITION. Decorate a special box with a removable lid for a gift you give to a family member, and start a traveling round robin–style tradition. The catch is that the box you give must be given to another family member the following year. By the time it reaches you, it just might be an heirloom.

CELEBRATING KWANZA. For a wonderful collection of ideas for celebrating Kwanza, purchase the book *A Kwanza Keepsake: Celebrating the Holiday with New Traditions & Feasts*, by Jessica B. Harris (Simon & Schuster, 1995).

TEA'S THE SEASON TO BE JOLLY. Put together a basket of gourmet flavored teas. This gift is certain to warm up anyone on your holiday gift list.

WARM WISHES. Send your warmest wishes with a basket filled with your favorite soup, gourmet coffee, or anything that will definitely warm someone up.

THANKSGIVING TREATS. Have a favorite turkey you are thankful for on your holiday gift list? Call 1-903-595-0725 weekdays and order a Greenberg's turkey. For fifty-eight years, Greenberg Smoked Turkeys have pleased a zillion people and more. You'll be thankful you know their turkeys!

GIVE THE GIFT OF GIVING. If you're giving someone money for the holidays, divide it into two gifts: one gift for them, and one for them to give to someone in need.

A HOLIDAY GIFT THAT WILL STACK UP. Call Happy Herman's at 1-800-825-6263 for a free gourmet gift guide filled with wonderful baskets and goodies. For more than forty-five years, this company has specialized in fabulous baskets and gourmet foods. Try the Georgia Nut-Stacker Trio of honey-roasted peanuts and pecans with a note that says, "Happy Holidays to someone we're nuts about!"

CELEBRATE! Call 1-800-CELEBRATE and order The Celebration Fantastic, a festive catalog filled with creative gifts for celebrating year-round.

HOLIDAY GIFTS AND MORE! Call 1-800-344-6125 and order the Sugar Hill Catalog. It's packed with gifts for spreading holiday joy!

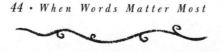

FOR A SPECIAL PAIR. Send a perfect holiday gift for a special pair on your gift list. Fill a colorful basket with pears and add a note that says, "Happy Holidays to a special pair!"

RING IN THE NEW YEAR. On New Year's Day, "ring" the people you care about most and let them know you value their presence in your life.

BEEN A GREAT YEAR? Put a bag or box of jelly beans in your favorite friends' mailboxes with a note that says, "Happy New Year! It's 'bean' a great year, thanks to you!"

4

Words of Sorrow

Each day should be passed as though it were our last.

—PUBLILIUS SYRUS

It's hard to know what to do, how to act, what to say, when someone is ill or has died. Some of the most difficult words to ever express are those of sorrow. Whether you are conveying your sympathy or sharing your feelings to comfort another, these words often matter most. Having experienced the loss of loved ones, far too often as I grow older, I have learned many an important lesson. During these trying times, words become the windows to the heart and really do make a difference.

Perhaps you have experienced a time in your life when friends and family reached out and embraced you with words and deeds that softened the pain you were feeling. While the hurt never left you, the spirit and caring that surrounded you comforted you in ways you never knew were possible. In these cases, the exchange of kind words helps both of you and caringly embraces you in your darkest hours.

In writing this chapter, I thought about a remarkable family whose child was a classmate of our daughter, Ali. When Ali was four years old, their little boy, Jonathan, stopped going to school because he had been diagnosed with cancer. Jonathan had experienced strong doses of radiation after brain surgery, and while he stayed confined to bed, his one wish was for Ali to come over and play.

When Jonathan heard she was coming he was ecstatic. As we arrived and rang the doorbell, Jonathan jumped out of bed and ran across the house to answer it. It was the first time he had gotten out of bed in weeks. As he and Ali sat down in the playroom to watch a movie, his mother said she felt she was chaperoning Jonathan's first and last date. That summer five-year-old Jonathan tragically lost his life to brain cancer.

This story is significant because it was Jonathan's mother who found an enormous amount of courage to console everyone else who didn't know what to say during this tragic time. She found words of thanks, words of courage, determination, kindness, to let everyone else know how much they had helped her family. When I asked Debbie what words, what deeds mattered most to her during those days, she said, "When someone you love is dying you feel as if you've crossed over the line. On one side of the line are the fortunate, the happy, the lucky, and on the other side are the doomed and the sick, where time moves slowly. The rest of the world is afraid of you."

Debbie said, "If you tell the world one thing, tell them never to err on the side of saying, 'I don't want to interfere, say the wrong thing,' or even 'They probably want to be left alone.' If you find yourself feeling this, move past it." Debbie added, "Say to yourself, 'I'm going to open the door and go to that person and if they want their isolation, that's fine.' But *never* assume that they don't need you. They are struggling. You can call up someone and say, 'I've been thinking of you,' but don't be afraid to talk about it. Write or tell them they're in your thoughts, you're thinking of them. Say, 'I'm so sorry,' and then listen to how they respond, but don't ever think they are being bombarded with too many thoughtful deeds."

Debbie also shared that we should keep in mind the anniversary dates and birthdays of the deceased. Any way that you can remember and keep their memory alive is important to a family. She added, "Always use the person's name; they want them to be remembered."

I then asked my aunt and uncle what helped them most when my cousin died. My aunt answered, "The people who really talked about Scott, special things they remembered about him, or things he did that were meaningful. That mattered most." In fact, they saved a selection of cards and letters that touched them in a beautiful way, each of which spoke directly about Scott's life rather than his death. My Aunt Lois pulled out of a drawer a special selection of letters and cards that she had saved and we tearfully reread them. Two years later, these words still had the same meaning, warmth, and love. They endured time, for each had illustrated a lesson filled with words that mattered, even two years after Scott's death.

Helpful Tips for Expressing Your Sympathy

When you don't know what to say, just say "I'm sorry, I care."

If you knew or know the person who is ill or has died, be sincere and write about their special traits that touched you. Recall something they taught you, or remember a deed they did. Your words will help personify their goodness and be more comforting than you'll ever know.

If you didn't know the deceased, you certainly know through their family how much they were loved. Take the

time to spell their name correctly. Be specific with your feelings and take the time necessary to say what's in your heart. Every thought counts.

When expressing your feelings to someone who has gone through a trauma, avoid saying, "I know how you feel." Unless you have walked in their shoes, simply acknowledge that you are thinking of them and are there if they should ever need you.

The following situations and chosen words will give you insight into ways to express yourself during trying times. These are simply some options; it's up to you to match your own feelings with the ones that suit you best.

When Someone Is Ill

Brevity is often the best advice for expressing your feelings to those who are ill. Whether or not you choose the perfect card, write a few of your own thoughts. A thoughtful reminder that you are thinking of them is what matters most. Small acts of kindness also make a significant difference—bringing in the mail, watering plants, taking a pet to the vet, having the oil in their car changed. It's the little things that count, and the person who makes a difference is one who finds out what someone really needs.

Shelley, a young woman facing cancer and a bone marrow transplant, wrote a beautiful letter to my friend Gail, who shared it with me. I felt compelled to share some of Shelley's advice that she sent her friends on how they could help her during her illness. She wrote:

Since I've become a "pro" at being a cancer survivor, allow me to give you some suggestions as to what other things besides prayer might be helpful to both you and me!

Just *seek* out a friend who is facing life challenges (not only cancer) in your area and pray for him or her, then call him or her and ask *specifically* what can you do for them today. I've had so much support, I can sincerely tell you how very comforting it is to have so many angels around me.

The help I've appreciated most has been the spur-of-the-moment kind. One friend came one day and just did my laundry; another cleaned out the refrigerator. I went six weeks not having to make a meal or be concerned about watching the children. After my surgery, I was too tired to take care of these details.

Or, if you are not comfortable with doing that (and some people aren't):

- Contact your local American Cancer Society and donate funds or time or transportation, whatever they need.
- Write or call me! Frankly, I'd love to hear from you, and writing me would probably be better, as then I can respond when I'm feeling energetic enough. I started chemotherapy in July and have had to be hospitalized for various infections, but I should be infection-free and ready to have the bone marrow transplant at the end of August.

- Please don't send fresh fruit or flowers, as I will be immuno-suppressed and those fresh things can have live germs which could infect me. Cards and prayers will do me lots of good.

  Lately, I just want to thank you for being part of my life. As you know, I'm not a very good writer, but one of my new life resolutions is to have more communication with those I love.

  SHELLEY

Shelley's words were very helpful to Gail since Shelley spoke frankly about her illness and how others could help her. Understanding the needs of the person who is ill is obviously a tremendous part of helping them. Often, though, we have no clue about what to do. I've never regretted the times I've sent a card or my wishes for someone's recovery, but I have learned over time that there is much more you can do if you really want to help. As you search for meaningful ways to comfort someone who is ill, choose from the following ideas or create your own, but keep in mind that illness requires respect. Ask your loved one or friend what he or she really needs, and listen and read between the lines. And remember, even if you can't be there, your words can.

Hope is the thing with feathers
That perches in the soul
And sings the tune without the words
And never stops, at all.

—EMILY DICKINSON

Dear ———,

I am hoping with every waking minute that you are finding a way to deal with your recent illness. I am here should you ever need anything at all, and my thoughts are with you, filled with love and wishes for your speedy recovery.

As I learned about your battle with breast cancer, I knew that it had no idea that it was dealing with such a tough cookie. You have been a source of strength for me my entire life, and I hope you will find the strength to deal with this difficult and trying time in a victorious manner.

If a gentle word
Could make your day
A little kinder
In any way,

I'd search for words
From A to Z
And sign each one
With love from me.

Dear ———,

I have realized throughout life that out of suffering and pain, somehow the strongest souls emerge. As you face your illness, I send hope that your suffering lessens and the depths of your strength embrace you, and offer you comfort in this difficult battle. I am sending you a strong dose of love.

Dear ———,

When I learned you were diagnosed with ———, I immediately wanted to reach out and hug you to let you know how much I care about you. You are such an important part of my life, and one of the kindest people I have ever known. I can only imagine that this must be the most difficult journey of your life. As you face this trying time, please know that you can count on me in any way.

MY LOVE ALWAYS,

Encourage children to make get-well cards with colorful drawings, and to express what they are feeling. Here's a perfect example of a message that accompanied a picture of a vase of flowers:

I am sorry Grandma you got picked out to be sick. Whoever did this really messed up.

—A SIX-YEAR-OLD BOY TO HIS GRANDMA

The Loss of a Loved One

During the past few years when my two cousins died tragically, I remember searching for the words to say as I reached into my heart and thought about what my cousins meant to me and how much they would be missed. I had fleeting hopes that I could support my aunts and uncles in some meaningful way during those difficult times as we all tried to make sense of their children's deaths.

From my discussion with many individuals who have lost a loved one, they all shared that it wasn't the words that were scripted, the ones that said, "You are in our hearts and prayers," it was the words that reflected the individual that mattered. It was those words describing meaningful moments that put the family closer to their loved one, even if only reminiscing for an instant. It was a good deed they did, a special story about them, a personality trait admired. It was as if those personalized words were a memorial to the lives lost, and each person who took the time to comment added a new chapter that made those life stories last one precious moment longer.

Of all the letters sent to my aunt and uncle when my cousin Scott died, one particular note that was saved mattered very much. It was about a kind deed no one would have ever known Scott did. These words were so precious, they became the greatest gift of all . . .

Dear Lois and Jerry,

I want to share a very special side of Scott's character with you. When my mother, Esther, had just about completely lost her sight and gardening was her only pleasure, she knew it was time to get someone to assist her. At this point she could not tell a flower from a weed. Fortunately she found Scott. He was a wonderful helper for what was to be the last summer she was able to work in the yard. As they worked side by side, I was amazed that someone this young was so exceptionally kind and patient. Mother trusted him completely and her garden flourished. He was a special kind of person who made that summer a happy one for Mother. Scott brought beauty to this world. I hope he is at peace in the other.

SINCERELY,
SONIA

Another condolence card of special meaning that was shared with me said:

.

There is a human bond that connects us all. It may be like a delicate thread, but in special times it becomes like a line of steel that helps to bind us, one to another.

This strand makes our sorrows more bearable, and in the long run that is what really matters. —— will be missed by his (her) family and his friends, but the thread of our human bonds will always keep some part of him (her) with you. I hope it will be an added source of comfort to you at this time of grief to know that others care.

MORE WORDS OF CONDOLENCE

Dear ——,

I once heard someone say that it's not death that brings us the greatest loss in life, but all that dies inside of us. As life goes on, I hope that you will find ways to celebrate the memory of your devoted mother. I know she

would want us all to live every day to the fullest and continue the celebration of her contagious love for life. May time speed your healing.

Passing time can never fade
All the special memories made;
Loved ones never really part
For they live inside your heart.

Dear ——,

I often thought that you followed in your father's every footstep. We all knew how much your Dad adored you, and we all send our deepest condolences. You made him the proudest dad on earth. I can recall all the times he spoke of you with pride and love. We have all lost a great friend, but in our hearts we know you have suffered the greatest loss of all. The heart has its own memory and we hope that in his memory you will discover the rich legacy he has left you and find comfort.

I hope the words that I might say
Could ease your pain in some small way.
May every thought sent to you
Give you strength to see it through.

Signatures for a Condolence Card

With every loving thought,

Our thoughts are with you at this time,

From the bottom of our hearts,

With heartfelt thoughts,

Your courage is an inspiration to all of us,

We feel fortunate to have known ——,

We hope your future will be complete with an abundance of happier times,

May your blessings be bountiful in the years to come,

I hope this time will pass quickly,

Take heart, brighter things are in store,

Sometimes there are no words that can reveal the feelings of the heart, but please accept my deepest thoughts of you during this time,

We join your large circle of friends and family who wish to bring you consolation during your time of grief,

May you find comfort in your fondest memories,

Another way to console someone is by a beautiful gesture. On the birthday of someone who has died, send a note to the family:

Dear ——,
—— has been on my mind lately and I know that his (her) birthday is on ——. I want you both to know that your family has blessed me in so many ways throughout the years with your concern for my well-being, and today I share the same concern for you. I have such warm and

happy memories of the times I spent with ——. I send my love to you and your family and want you to know that —— will live eternally in my heart.

MUCH LOVE,

When Someone Has Experienced a Tragedy

Tragedies pierce the heart in every direction. Often some unexpected, inexcusable circumstance causes a family or individual pain. A drunk driver, a freak accident, a fire—the tragedies bombard us on the news every day. It's hard to believe that they could ever hit home. My friend Steve shared a touching story with me about his friend and coworker Dennis, who came to see him in a theatrical performance. Dennis insisted they go out for dessert in Steve's honor after the play.

Steve recalled it as if it were yesterday. He told me, "On Dennis's way home, a twenty-six-mile drive, when he and his wife were one block away from their home, a speeding car broadsided the driver's seat. After days in a coma, Dennis died." Steve added, "I soul-searched for days when he died, but the one thing I learned that I think about often is what did I admire most about Dennis? In his case, it was his persistence and commitment to doing things well. Anytime I do anything important, I think of Dennis's commitment to excellence and try to keep his spirit alive by honoring that trait. It's how he lived his life, and he has inspired me to try harder in his memory."

The following paragraph is similar to what Steve now writes as he pays his condolences to someone after a tragedy:

While there are no words I can say that might help you during this difficult time, I thought of something that has helped me and might be of comfort to you. I encourage you to think of one thing that you admired and loved most about your loved one, and in a tribute to their memory, keep their spirit alive by acknowledging it in your life.

Here are other condolence cards that were sent after a tragic death and saved through the years and treasured:

Dear ——,

From the moment we heard of ——'s death, you and the family have been in our thoughts constantly. How does a family cope with such a tragedy? How can anyone who has not suffered such pain bring any measure of comfort or solace? We do not have the answers to either question.

But you have helped those of us who cherish your friendship and love. You and the family have exhibited a spiritual and physical strength that has allowed us to mourn with you. The multitude of people who came to call is certainly a tribute to —— and to the understanding, love, and support he received from all of you throughout his life.

We hope that each day will be a bit brighter, and that your lives will return to the normal and mundane. You are truly blessed with your children, grandchildren, family, and extended family; your host of friends.

We feel fortunate to have known —— all these years and to have seen the fruits of his creativity and sensitivity.

Physically —— is no longer among us, but surely the legacy of his warmth and his talent will endure forever.

WITH LOVE,

Dear ——,

There is no way we can comprehend your recent tragedy, and we know it has left you searching for answers that might be difficult to ever find. Please know that in your darkest hour, your pain touches all of us and we mourn your loss as if it were our own.

Dear ——,

——'s recent accident has caused us all to think of you constantly, and we send our condolences and deepest thoughts to comfort you during this tragic time. ——'s death was senseless, and we want you to know how much she will be missed. She had a special way of making everyone feel at home whenever in her presence. We hope you will find the strength to deal with your pain, and please know how deeply we feel for you at this time.

Dear——,

From what I have experienced and learned over the years, I can earnestly say that most of the questions—the why's and what-if's—are likely to remain unanswered. I think it will be the best use of your thought and energy to remember the pleasant aspects of ——'s life rather than to dwell on the tragic circumstances. May the time be hurried so all your memories will be good ones.

Give a Gift in Someone's Memory

A meaningful way to honor the memory of someone is to make a contribution to a worthwhile cause in their name. Find a nonprofit organization in your area or choose one of the following, and ask them to send an acknowledgment card or tribute card in memory of the deceased. This act of kindness says so much, especially when you choose a cause that would have been meaningful to that person.

Here are some suggestions:

Pediatric Aids Foundation: 1-800-488-5000 or
1-310-395-9051

American Cancer Society: 1-800-227-2345

Child Abuse Prevention Services:
Good/Touch–Bad/Touch: 1-800-245-1527

Susan G. Komen Breast Cancer Foundation:
1-800-I'M-AWARE (1-800-462-9273)

Prevent Blindness America: 1-800-331-2020

American Heart Association: 1-800-AHA-USA1
(1-800-242-8721)

American Foundation for AIDS Research (AmFAR):
1-800-39-AmFAR (1-800-392-6327)

Audrey Hepburn Hollywood for Children Foundation:
1-800-KIDS-818

Acknowledging Condolences

When Helen Cavalier, a very special woman, passed away, her family sent a meaningful poem similar to this one to acknowledge the condolences they'd received.

Dear Friends & Family,

Perhaps you sent a lovely card
  Or sat quietly in a chair.
Perhaps you sent a contribution
  Or brought food to show you care.

Perhaps you called or spoke as kind a word
  As any friend could say.
Perhaps you came by our home
  And spent some time one day.

Whatever you did to console the heart,
Our thanks to you for your special part.

THE FAMILY OF _____

5

Words of Apology

You cannot shake hands with a clenched fist.

—INDIRA GANDHI

Saying You're Sorry

"I'm sorry." Often we forget how important these words are, but over time they still remain very powerful and important. Sometimes our apologies are for little things, other times for when we really blew it! There are some actions that are never worth forgetting but always worth forgiving. And there are other situations that we find simply unforgivable. However, I'm always amazed at how people work things out when they really care about each other.

Over the years, I have always cared about hearing someone else's opinion to see if there is something I'm not comprehending. I also believe that when we welcome a difference of opinion, we grow and learn how to tolerate and eventually understand each other, as well as ourselves.

I love to be right. Who doesn't? But being right doesn't always mean we're sensitive and kind and loving. Being those things is often more important than being right. That's not to say you should ever compromise your values. You shouldn't. But life is short and regret can be painful. So think of someone to whom you owe an apology or whom you haven't forgiven. Perhaps it's because of some ridiculous ceremony on which you're standing. Or you think they should apologize first. If you apologize and they don't accept it, if you really mean it, don't give up. Learn from it, understand it, and walk hand in hand with the conflict until you have come to some resolution. This may mean walking away from the situation for a while. But always do what's in your heart and hopefully your words will make a difference.

There are many ways to say you're sorry. If you really are, don't give up . . . try these first!

SEND AN APOLOGY AND BE SPECIFIC

Dear ——,

I am writing to express my sincerest apologies for hurting your feelings. When I said you are not a caring friend, I should have thought of all the times you've been there for me. My actions were never intended to negate all the years you have stood by my side. I have obviously hurt you deeply, and I regret speaking without thinking first.

Sometimes my brain and mouth just aren't attached. If there is anything I can say or do, I'd go to any lengths to express my remorse. I only hope you will find a way to let me back in your thoughts in a gentler way. My deepest apologies. I'm sorry.

Dear ——,

In principle, I have always believed that hurting another person's feelings was something I am not capable of. But in this instance, I have hurt yours. My actions were unacceptable and I have labored over how I could ever have done such an insensitive thing.

I know I cannot retract my actions, but I hope I can make it up to you with a heartfelt apology. I have learned a lesson from this experience, and thanks to you I think I will be a more sensitive person.

Dear ——,

You have given me the gift of forgiveness, and while I will always be sorry for hurting your feelings, I want you to know how deeply appreciative I am that you allowed me to learn such a sacred lesson at your expense. I'm truly sorry for what I said, and value the gracious and endearing way in which you expressed your feelings. I am really sorry.

Dear ——,

"It is not best that we should all think alike; it is difference of opinion which makes horse races." This quote from Mark Twain suggests that each of our opinions matters, and it is in this spirit that I owe you an apology. I often see my opinion as the only one, and in this case I ignored your feelings and rejected your valuable ideas. I only hope you will accept my apology for jumping the gate with such a closed mind, and allow me the chance to hear your opinions again soon.

Dear ——,

"The only good is knowledge and the only evil is ignorance."—Socrates. Based on the lessons I have learned from knowing you, I feel I have grown to learn more about what really matters. No longer can I remain indifferent to your feelings. Please accept my apology, as I re-

main very sorry for anything I have done that has exhibited an unflattering ignorance on my part.

Dear ——,

Somehow we forget the years but remember the moments. I remember all the reasons I've been upset with you for years, but to my surprise they have slowly lost their meaning. I now fear that the time will come when I'll be too proud to tell you I'm sorry that we've lost so much time together and grown apart. I have always cared about you and your well-being, and while I have stood on a silly principle for so long, I have always held your happiness in my thoughts. I am sorry for all the time we've lost. Is there any way to start again and rediscover our friendship?

More Words That Say "I'm Sorry"

The best thinking has been done in solitude. The worst has been done in turmoil.

—THOMAS ALVA EDISON

Everything that irritates us about others can lead us to an understanding of ourselves.

—CARL JUNG

Honesty is the first chapter of the book of wisdom.

—THOMAS JEFFERSON

*It's hard to look pleasant when anguish is present
And yet it is strictly worthwhile,
Not all of your scowling and fussing and growling
Can show off your grit like a smile.*

—WALTER MACON

It does not require many words to speak the truth.

—CHIEF JOSEPH

A fanatic is one who can't change his mind and won't change the subject.

—WINSTON CHURCHILL

CLEVER WAYS TO SAY "I'M SORRY"

HAVE A HEART. Send heart-shaped candies with a note that says, "I'm sorry I ate your heart out."

AN APPEALING APOLOGY. Bag up onions and send a note that says, "I'm sorry . . . You'll never cry over me again, only these."

FULL OF HOT AIR? Send a bouquet of balloons with a note that says, "I'm sorry . . . I blew it!"

SEND A FAN LETTER. Apologize by sending a portable desk-top fan with a note that says, "I was full of hot air . . . please forgive me."

SORRY YOU BLURTED SOMETHING OUT? Send a jar or bag of screws with a note that says, "Sorry, I really screwed up!"

MAD ABOUT YOU? Send a copy of *Mad* magazine with a note saying, "Don't stay *Mad* at me forever . . . I'm sorry." Or better yet, "Who, me worry? You bet I do. I'm sorry . . . please call me soon!"

OPPOSITES ATTRACT. Send a magnet with a poem: "Opposites attract, but we shouldn't fight; I hope you *steel* love me, you were absolutely right!"

SALT AND PEPPER. Wrap up a pair of salt and pepper shakers with a bit of verse: "We go together like pepper and salt; Please forgive me, it was all my fault!"

BUBBLING WITH AN APOLOGY? Wrap up a bottle of bubble bath or bubbles with a card that says, "I'm sorry if I burst your bubble!"

GOING BANANAS. Try saying you're sorry by wrapping up a bunch of bananas or even banana bread with a note that says, "I'm sorry I made you bananas" or "I'll go bananas if you don't accept my apology!"

IN THE DOGHOUSE? Wrap up a dog bone or box of dog biscuits with this note: "I hope you'll let me out of the doghouse soon! I'm doggone sorry!"

GET THE POINT. Send a jar filled with pins and needles and a card that says, "I'll be walking on pins and needles until you forgive me!"

Just in Case You're Late . . .

I have a reason
For being so late;
I simply forgot
The day and the date.
I feel just awful,
I've shed many a tear;
I hope you'll forgive me . . .
And then remind me next year.

6

♥

Words of Congratulation

Write it in your heart that every day is the best day
of the year.

—RALPH WALDO EMERSON

All year long there are many reasons to say "Congratulations!" and
around the world every country has a special way to say it. In Hebrew
it's "Mazel tov!," in Spanish it's "Felicidades!," and in Portuguese
it's "Parabens!" While the words change, the message stays the same.
From wedding congratulations to graduations, acknowledging another's happiness or accomplishment is always appreciated. Here are
some clever ways to express your feelings:

Weddings

CONGRATULATE THEM IN RHYME

A wedding day is filled with love
And happiness times two,
And all the joy that life can offer
We send to both of you.

Wishing you years of love
And special times to treasure.
This special day belongs to you—
May your happiness last forever.

CLEVER MESSAGES TO ENCLOSE WITH WEDDING OR SHOWER GIFTS

China that is registered: May your happiness be registered forever!

A picture frame: May your life together be picture perfect! (Enclose their wedding invitation in the frame.)

Crystal: It's crystal clear you two are a perfect match!

A piece of art: To an original couple!

A blender: You're a perfect blend!

An appliance: We're glad you discovered the electricity between you!

A pair of candlesticks: May your love shine forever!

A personalized door knocker: May happiness always knock at your door!

A teapot: You suit each other to a "tea"!

CALLING ALL BRIDES. Call 1-800-82-BRIDE (1-800-822-7433) and register your favorite bride at the Ross-Simons Bridal Registry. You can also get a free catalog filled with fine jewelry, tableware, and collectibles by calling 1-800-556-7376. Ross-Simon's value-pricing reflects savings of 20 to 70 percent off comparative retail prices on most items, and the bridal registry offers a free gift wrap for registered brides. This is a great tip for anyone you know getting married since the company carries an extensive line of china and tableware.

Creative Anniversary Gifts

BE CREATIVE IN YOUR DELIVERY. My husband has always been the most creative and romantic of all when it comes to celebrating our anniversary. One year Willy gave me a bracelet in the head of a puppet, and another year I received a watch that was stuffed in the back of a teddy bear in which a Velcro opening had been sewn.

GOT THE HOTS? Send a container filled with cinnamon red hots with a note that says, "I've got the hots for you!"

1-800-FLOWERS. Call 1-800-356-9377 to send beautiful fresh flowers. The company offers a variety of gift baskets, plants and topiaries, chocolate candies, balloons, and delightful desserts. They even have a Blooming Plant of the Month Club that entitles the forgetful gift-giver to send a thoughtful present to someone special every month and only have to remember to do it once. Call them 24 hours a day, 365 days a year, or reach them through the Internet (http://www.800flowers.com). All products are backed by a 100 percent customer service guarantee. Add words such as "Beautiful flowers remind me of you," or send sunflowers and say, "You are my sunshine."

WALKING ON AIR? Send balloons and include one of these messages: "I'm ten feet off the ground because you love me!" or "I'm walking on air because I'm married to you!"

SEND CHOCOLATES. Send anything chocolate with a note that says, "There's no one sweeter than you!"

ADD SOME SPICE. Fill a basket with a selection of spices. Add a note saying, "You spice up my life!"

HEAD OVER HEELS IN LOVE? Send a pair of flip-flops with a special note that reads, "I flipped over you the second we met!"

ANNIVERSARY GIFTS—A YEAR AT A GLANCE

1st year	Paper, plastic
2nd	Cotton, china
3rd	Leather
4th	Linen, silk
5th	Wood
6th	Iron
7th	Copper
8th	Bronze
9th	Pottery
10th	Tin, aluminum
11th	Steel
12th	Linen, silk
13th	Lace
14th	Ivory

15th	Crystal, glass
20th	China
25th	Silver
30th	Pearl
35th	Jade, coral
40th	Ruby, garnet
45th	Sapphire
50th	Gold
55th	Emerald, turquoise
60th	Diamond
75th	Diamond

A New Baby

WELCOME THE NEWCOMER WITH A RHYME

We are so happy
We are filled with joy . . .
Welcome! Welcome!
To your baby boy!

A baby is the greatest gift
That anyone can know;
Your hearts are filled with endless love
And every day it grows;
So please accept our wishes
As parents you now start
A brand-new place where love will grow
That begins inside your heart.

Babies do so many things:
They make you laugh, they make you sing,
They keep you up all night long,
They're very cute, they do no wrong;
Their needs could fill up any list,
And when they want you, they will persist.
They take up time—all you've got;
They're very expensive and cost a lot,
They try your patience, want every toy,
But with a baby comes the greatest joy!

That precious baby, such an adorable face,
Will melt you into a basket case.
But if you see you're growing pale,
It's probably thanks to the endless wails.

Roses are red
Violets are blue,
There's nothing a baby
Can't get you to do!

Congratulations, dear friend of mine,
You're about to encounter a memorable time.
Becoming a parent is a big job to do . . .
So call me when the baby's due!

ORDER A TIME CAPSULE. Call 1-800-729-8463. The Original Time Capsule Company will help you capture a special time! Order a time capsule for your baby or for a newborn to whom you wish to send a special gift. It's a wonderful way to save special words or mementos, and a clever gift that will always be treasured. Add a note that says, "Like this time capsule, may your new baby fill your lives with endless amounts of joy and happiness."

A New Job

Celebrate someone's success with a creative congratulations.

SEND A QUOTE. Send a card with a meaningful quote such as "Success is a journey, not a destination" (Ben Sweetland).

WRITE A LETTER.

> Dear ——,
> We are fired up with enthusiasm about your new job! Your accomplishment is well-deserved, and we knew you could do it. We wish you years filled with success and all the good fortune that life has to offer.

HERE'S A GIFT WITH APPEAL! Welcome a new employee to the bunch or congratulate a top banana with an actual bunch of bananas. Use a permanent felt-tip pen and write the person's name all over the bunch. Add a colorful bow and you're ready to go!

CREATIVE NEW-JOB GIFTS

GIVE A CLOCK.

> *Time flies when you're having fun.*
> *Congratulations on a job well done.*

WRAP UP A ROLL OF STAMPS. You're on a roll! Congratulations! Or: You have earned our stamp of approval!

PIGGY BANK. Hope you break the bank! Congratulations!

PAPERWEIGHT. This job was worth "weighting" for. Congratulations!

A New Home

When someone moves into a new house, "move" them with a creative welcome.

SEND A RHYME

We heard you moved to a new home.
For you, we're quite excited;
We hope that you'll be settled soon
And soon we'll be invited!

Closet to closet,
Room to room,
To your beautiful home
We will come soon.

Inside your house
May happiness rest,
And through the years
Your family be blessed.

CLEVER GIFTS FOR THE NEW HOUSE

PERSONALIZE IT! A new address is always in need of mono-grammed stationery, return-address labels, or anything with the new address. Make a stationery kit filled with the stationery, stamps, and tools for writing notes, and add a note that says, "May good news be abundant in your new home."

HOME SWEET HOME. Send a basket of sweets to someone who just moved into a new home. Add a note saying, "No matter where you ever roam, may you have a Home Sweet Home.

Retirement

SEND A POEM

To a successful life you have aspired,
And now it's time that you retire;
We're proud of you and the legacy you gave us—
And while you're out fishing (playing golf, etc.), be sure to
*   wave to us!*

Over the hills and valley you go,
To retirement land, oh no, oh no!
Knowing you are a real self-starter,
You'll probably end up working much harder!

CREATIVE RETIREMENT GIFTS

Give the Following with an Accompanying Card

Beach chair: Life's a beach—enjoy it!

Hammock: Put your feet up—you deserve it!

Magazine subscription: Choose a subscription that reflects their interest and say, "Now read this! You finally have time!"

Send Your Congrats in Memo Form

TO: ALL RETIREES
FROM: (YOUR NAME)
RE: MANDATORY INSTRUCTIONS FOR LIFE
WORK ORDER: HAVE A HAPPY LIFE FILLED WITH
    JOY, FAMILY, PEACE, AND FULFILLMENT.
TIME REQUIREMENTS: WORK ON THIS DAILY!
MESSAGE: YOU EARNED IT! ENJOY IT!

Graduation

SEND POETIC CONGRATULATIONS

Dear Graduate,
You've paid your dues and now it's time
To go to college and end this rhyme.
So here's to you and all the fun you've had . . .
We're still amazed that you're a grad!

A graduate: did we hear
You've ended high school's final year?
We wish you luck and much success;
Good luck at college . . . do your best!

CREATIVE GRADUATION GIFTS

CREATE AN I-CARE PACKAGE. If you have a college-bound grad on your list, fill a laundry basket or bag with the basics, from sheets to shampoo, cookies to clocks. These dorm room necessities will definitely be put to good use!

TAKING STOCK IN THE FUTURE. Give a grad a stock related to their specific area of interest. Wrap it up in the Stock Exchange page of the newspaper for a clever presentation!

PICTURE THIS. Enclose a picture of the graduate with a note that says, "We're 'grad' you made it!"

GIVE AN UPDATED DICTIONARY. Attach a note that reads, "May you always have the final word!"

MAKE A POINT! Call 1-800-995-4810 and order the Montblanc catalog for the discriminating buyer. These elegant pens are the "write" gift for your favorite graduate. Wrap it up with personalized note cards and address one to you so the graduate can stay in touch!

7

Words of Love

I like not only to be loved, but to be told I am
loved.

—GEORGE ELIOT

I try never to miss an opportunity to tell someone that I care about
them. I realize how short life is and always try to celebrate and value
the love in my life. And by constantly reinforcing our love, we give
ourselves the opportunity to stay in touch with those who matter most
of all. My parents have taught me this by example. They almost never
end a conversation without saying "I love you," and I realize how
blessed I am to have such a loving family.

There are so many ways to tell someone you love them. My husband tells me he loves me by saying it, and also by filling my car with
gas. While that isn't romantic, it sure saves me time and keeps me
going! A kiss, a hug, an "I love you" just touch the tip of the iceberg
when it comes to expressing love. So don't forget, and don't procras-
tinate; tell the people in your life whom you care about that you love
them.

The following quotes and words of love are yours for the choosing.
Use them to inspire your imagination as you connect with those you
love, and keep in mind it's the little things you do or say that matter
most.

Quotes of Love

All that I am or hope to be I owe to my mother.

—ABRAHAM LINCOLN

Personally, the only four-letter word I would use is Love.

—MAE WEST

Love is willing to endure
All that fortune cannot cure.
And since sorrows must be had,
Love is happy to be sad.

—EDGAR A. GUEST

And I say there is nothing greater than the mother of men.

—WALT WHITMAN

The way to give advice to your children is to find out what they want and then advise them to do it.

—HARRY S. TRUMAN

I have found the paradox that if I love until it hurts, then there is no hurt, but only more love.

—MOTHER TERESA

She was as good as she was fair,
None, none on earth above her!
As pure in thoughts as angels are—
To know her was to love her.

—SAMUEL ROGERS

Happy is he that is happy in his children.

—ENGLISH PROVERB

Lovers alone wear sunlight.

—E.E. CUMMINGS

'Tis better to have loved and lost than never to have loved
at all.

—ALFRED, LORD TENNYSON

Love is what you have been through with somebody.

—JAMES THURBER

Love adds a precious seeing to the eye.

—WILLIAM SHAKESPEARE

Came but for friendship / And took away love.

—THOMAS MOORE

There are only two lasting bequests we can give our
children. One is roots, the other is wings.

—ANONYMOUS

Love is the gift of oneself.

—JEAN ANOUILH

Love is looking together in the same direction.

—ANTOINE DE SAINT-EXUPÉRY

Brief is life but long is love.

—ALFRED, LORD TENNYSON

In our family an experience was not finished, not truly
experienced, unless written down or shared with another.

—ANNE MORROW LINDBERGH

Where love is concerned, too much is not enough.

—PIERRE-AUGUSTIN DE BEAUMARCHAIS

I lived for those who love me / Whose hearts are kind
and true.
—GEORGE LINNAEUS BANKS

My creed is love and you are its only tenet.
—JOHN KEATS

The supreme happiness of life is the conviction that we
are loved.
—VICTOR HUGO

If you judge people, you have no time to love them.
—MOTHER TERESA

Take away love and our earth is a tomb.
—ROBERT BROWNING

Where we love, we always have something to say.
—LADY MARY WORTLEY MONTAGU

Love keeps the cold out better than a cloak.
—HENRY WADSWORTH LONGFELLOW

A loving heart is the truest wisdom.
—CHARLES DICKENS

For Your Children

Children, like all of us, need to hear words of love in many ways.
These words work best when said over and over, and also when expressed creatively. Don't forget that even if your children are grown,
they still need to hear them, too. There are many ways to say "I love
you" to a child; here are some to get you started.

CREATE A POEM FOR YOUR CHILD

To my child:
Oh my precious child,
I want you to remember
All the happy times we've had
From January to December;
Every day you've learned
Something special and new,
But one thing's for sure
And that's I love you.

Dear Daughter,
A daughter is someone special—
No matter what, she's there;
And when she's ever needed,
She always shows she cares;
She's totally dependable,
Quite witty and very charming;
She always keeps her cool—that is,
Unless something is alarming;
A daughter is someone special—
You love her from the start;
A daughter is a precious soul,
For she lives inside your heart.

Dear Son,
Some sons are quite ingenious,
Considerate and kind;

Some sons are quite creative,
As clever as you'll find;
Some sons are quite amazing—
This fact is really true;
And what a joy it is for us
Since all these things are you!

CREATE AN I-LOVE-YOU STORY
WITH YOUR CHILD

Quite often, our daughter, Ali, and I play a little game with an open-ended story. We alternate who says each line and it goes like this . . .

I love you more than the tallest mountain,
And then some.
I love you more than the deepest ocean,
And then some.

And then here's what happens . . .

I love you more than the tallest chocolate ice cream,
And then some.
I love you more than the most gigantic skyscraper on earth,
And then some.

We take turns saying each part, and the story grows on and on and on . . .

COMPOSE A SONG

You need not be a musician, but here's an idea you might want to tune in to. When our children were born, I wrote both of them a song and put it in their baby book. Justin's began like this:

> *Just for Justin, yessireee,*
> *He's the sunshine, just for me.*
> *Oh Justin, I'm bustin' with love . . .*

And Ali's started like this:

> *We're singing in the daylight;*
> *Everything is all right,*
> *Ali, thanks to you . . .*

Your turn!

WHEN YOUR CHILD IS GROWN

> *Dear ——,*
> *Of the happiest times in my entire life*
> *Were times when you were small;*
> *Teaching you about the world*
> *Was really best of all;*
> *And now as we grow older,*
> *We haven't changed our ways,*
> *For when we're spending time together—*
> *They're still my favorite days.*

Dear ——,
When I became your parent,
I was overwhelmed with joy—
I was such a proud parent
Of a bouncing baby boy!
When I became your parent,
It was the greatest gift of all—
Watching you learn to walk and talk
And jump and grow so tall!
And now you are a parent,
And this I must confide—
I still count my blessings daily
For my gifts have multiplied.

For Your Parents

Of all the words I've ever said,
Keep these beside your heart,
In case we're not together
Or find ourselves apart:
My deepest thoughts begin and end
Each day with thoughts of you;
It starts and stops with this one thought,
And that is . . . I love you!

GIVE AN AWARD

To the world's greatest parents:
You've won a big award,
For all the times you entertained me
When I was really bored;
You fed and clothed and taught me,
Everything I could need;
You shared with me your wisdom,
So that I would succeed;
And all I am I owe to you,
And on this day bestow
The World's Greatest Parent Award—
To both of you it goes!

DEAR MOTHER OR FATHER

Dearest Mother (Father), where do I begin?
You mean so much to me;
To put my love into these words
Is hard as it can be;
So please remember always
That since the very start,
I've loved you more than life itself
And that's straight from my heart.

Sometimes I forget to say
How much I really care.
Instead I ask and ask and plea . . .
Please, take me here and there.
You'd think that I'd know better,
I'd clean up once in a while,
But Mom (Dad), you're always there for me
With your patient, understanding smile.
So Mom (Dad), I wrote this poem
To say thanks for all you do.
I hope that when I grow up,
I turn out just like you.

For Your Family

Grandma and Grandpa,
What can I say?
I love you both
In every possible way.
You've taught me so much
You're grand as they come,
And one thing's for sure . . .
You know how to have fun!

Why, you ask, are we all fussin'?
We've got the greatest family of cousins,
Uncles and aunts, nephews and nieces—
We totally adore each other to pieces.
From Atlanta to Tennessee,
We're a family, yes, we'll always be.

No matter what happens, you can plainly see
We're glad we grew on this family tree.

Whenever I count my blessings
It's very plain to see,
That all of my many blessings
Begin with my family.
So here's a little poem,
I hope you'll think it's swell.
When someone asks if we're related,
Don't you ever, ever tell!
(Just kidding)

For Your Significant Other

There are folks who find it hard to say,
I love you each and every day.
But since it's true, I must say,
I love you more each passing day.

Love doesn't just make the world go round,
It's the greatest trip for which we're bound.
How lucky I am throughout my life
You've been on board as my wife.

Dear ——,

   You are an angel without wings, for you seem to be
there for me at every turn. You understand and anticipate
my every thought, and I feel blessed and certain that we
were destined to be together.

Understanding you is never easy—
This statement is quite true;
But loving you is without question
The best thing I could do.

Dear ——,
Of all the words I've ever said,
Keep these beside your heart
For when we cannot be together
And find ourselves apart:
My deepest thoughts begin and end
Each day that I may weather
With thoughts of you and this simple thought—
I love you and that's forever.

I may not say I love you
As often as I should,
So I'm sending you this rhyme
To remind me that I should.
In case I haven't said it,
I love you, yes I do . . .
No matter where you ever go,
I'll always be with you.

Creative I-Love-Yous

CREATE AN I-LOVE-YOU BOOK. Get a blank journal and record in it often all the special things about your child or loved one. Our friend Mark does this with his daughter Naomi, and they take turns! This little book of little thoughts will be treasured forever. Be

sure to always put the date; that way you'll be certain to capture each precious moment in time.

MAKE AN I-LOVE-YOU BOX. Search for the perfect box or chest and make a Heart Box for your child. I found an old silverware box in the shape of a heart, and lined it with satin for our daughter Ali. I saved her first shoes and socks, rattle, and so forth in this box and we call it the heart box. It's filled with special and meaningful mementos that touched our hearts and are priceless to us.

PILLOW TALK. Leave a special poem or "I love you" on your child's or significant other's pillow. If ever you can't be there, leave a rain check for a hug and kiss good night.

HAVE AN ALI DAY. Make your child feel special with a special day in her or his honor. Surprise your child with a special movie. Visit the library, have a picnic, climb a tree, and end it with this poem:

> *Of any girl (boy), I couldn't be fonder,*
> *That's why this day is in your honor.*
> *Wherever we go and whatever we do,*
> *Remember this day, it says* I love you.

WRITE "I LOVE YOU" IN LIPSTICK. Just like in the movies, try it! Just do it once . . . they'll never forget it, and be sure to seal it with a kiss!

SEND A PIZZA. Order a pizza and send it to the door of someone you love with a note that says, "Here's a 'pizza' my heart!'

GIVE A MUSIC BOX. Call 1-800-227-2190 and order a free catalog from the San Francisco Music Box Company. Purchase a music box that plays a special song that would be meaningful. Create a clever note and tape it onto the bottom of the box so it'll always be there with love from you! Many of the company's musical gifts, from picture frames to paperweights, can be customized with a favorite song. Suggested songs of love: "I Will Always Love You" or "Unforgettable."

LOTTERY TICKETS. Give a lottery ticket to someone you love with a note that says, "I'm a winner because I love you!"

SWEET TALK. Fill her purse or his briefcase with their favorite candy and attach a note saying, "No one's sweeter than you!"

SAY "I LOVE YOU" IN ANOTHER LANGUAGE. Choose some other language in which to say "I love you" and add a note: "I love you in every language!"

French: *Je t'aime*

Chinese: *Wo ai nei*

Spanish: *Te amo*

CHECKMATE. Write a check to your loved one for one thousand kisses or two million hugs. Fill in what the check is for: "Just because I love you!" Sign your name and the date.

TAPE IT. Record a poem or letter to your loved one. Kids love these, especially when going away to camp. Or, if you're a traveling parent, this is a great idea for staying connected.

SEND YOUR LOVE IN A CREATIVE WAY. Combine your love-ly thoughts with a creative gift. Here are some clever ideas to get you started:

Oreo cookies: I'm a smart cookie because I love you!

Assortment of pencils: Get the point . . . I love you!

Coffee cup: My cup runneth over, thanks to you!

Golf tees: You suit me to a tee!

Almond Joy candy: You fill my life with joy!

P.S. I LOVE YOU. Send a sheet or even a single Love stamp with a note that says, "P.S., I love you . . . write soon!" You could also leave the stamps in your loved one's briefcase or drawer with a personalized note: "You're stamped in my heart forever!"

JUST FOR ME TV. Tape a zillion hours of your loved one's favorite television shows! This works beautifully if they love talk shows and they are at work all day. From Oprah to the morning shows, these hours will be especially meaningful when thoughtfully chosen.

TAPE-RECORDED LAUGHTER. Record the laughter of someone you love. This makes a wonderful gift for parents or grandparents. What a special sound you'll always have preserved!

FRAME A SPECIAL MEMORY. Frame a special item for a loved one, from the bat or ball from their first home run or hit to the playbill from a special evening. I've framed everything from our daughter's first dress to my grandmother's purse. They not only look beautiful but preserve a special memory that will be cherished for generations.

PICTURE THIS. With the exciting new technology in photography, you can now have a photograph re-created on a variety of ob-

jects, from mugs to calendars to T-shirts. You can also manipulate a photo and add or delete a person. Photographs are the perfect way to say "I Love You!" A company called Wolf Camera & Video has this service as well as a fabulous catalog. Call 1-800-643-WOLF to request one, or find the location nearest you.

WRITE A LOVE LETTER. Don't forget how! Write a love letter just like old times. It'll be treasured forever.

NUMBERS THAT MATTER. Show how much you love someone with information that might matter in an emergency. Provide a list of telephone numbers in an address book and include important numbers such as poison control, etc. For a loved one who has a special circumstance, you could also include 1-800 numbers that might be important resources or provide helpful information to them. Be sure to include a note that says, "If you need me, call me!"

GRIN AND BEAR IT. Call 1-800-829-BEAR if you can't bear to live without someone. Tell the person so creatively by sending a teddy bear from the Vermont Teddy Bear Company. Gift-givers can send a Bear-Gram, which includes a personalized message. Prices start at $52 for a 15-inch bear and the price varies depending on the size and outfit.

AMAZING PASTA-BILITIES. Call 1-800-449-2121. Here's an edible way to say "I Love You!" Hittin the Trail is an innovative catalog from Buckeye Beans & Herb, Inc., a company that specializes in custom pasta and super soups. Their pasta comes in the shape of footballs, musical notes (sure to hit a chord with your love interest), and, best of all, there's a romantic pasta that comes in the shape of hearts. Show how much you care with this sweetheart of a gift!

Clever sayings: "I won't pasta through life without you!" "The pasta-bilities for us are endless!"

IN THE SPIRIT OF LOVE. Call 1-800-220-ROSE for one of the most fabulous catalogs filled with a beautiful selection of meaningful gifts. The Red Rose Collection has something for everyone on your gift list who has heart!

DOES SOMEONE SUIT YOU TO A T? Call 1-800-298-4-TEA and order The Republic of Tea, a catalog specializing in full-leaf teas and herb blends, plus a tea-riffic selection of teatime products from tea books to tea-shirts.

GOT THE HOTS FOR SOMEONE? Call 1-800-GREAT-SW (1-800-473-2879) to order the Great Southwest Cuisine catalog and discover a really hot selection of edible gifts, from Viper Venom Salsa to Hot Stuff BBQ to a Hot Pasta Basket. This catalog is definitely for those who are too hot to handle.

COLD FEET, WARM HEART? Here's the perfect gift for someone you love. Step right up and order the Acorn Products catalog at 1-800-872-2676. Check out their unbelievable fleece sock selection, guaranteed to warm up cold feet!

JUST CALL AND SAY "I LOVE YOU." Every hour on the hour, call someone you love and tell them. Your words will be ringing in their ears!

PICTURE PERFECT. When framing a photograph, add a special note to the back of the frame that identifies the subject, gives the date, and says something special about the person pictured. Generations to come will treasure your words.

8

Words of Friendship

And I can live my life on earth contented to the end,
If but a few shall know my worth
And proudly call me friend.

—EDGAR A. GUEST

Friends sweeten life's pleasures and soften life's sorrows. I am fortunate to have wonderful friends who would come to my rescue and slay dragons, if necessary. And my friends know, too, I would do the same for them. Letting your friends know you love and appreciate them reconfirms their faith that they are being a good friend.

I believe that friends are life's greatest treasures. Over the years I have watched my mother and her best friend from college maintain a long-distance friendship. Every time Mom goes to New York, the highlight of her trip is seeing Joan. You'd think they were in college all over again. Staying in touch with friends is a lifelong gift you can give to yourself. Sometimes it's as easy as organizing your friends' telephone numbers and special dates and having them right by your telephone or bedside.

When it comes to friends, you must act on your generous impulses and kind thoughts, and you'll be surprised how many new friends you might even discover! Whether a friend is celebrating, commiserating, enjoying, annoying, debating, divorcing, thoughtful, thought-less—remember that they still are your friend. Lead them by example, teach them by being honest, and welcome and treasure them in your life. Friends matter more than you will ever know, for they choose your company for now and sometimes for life.

Quotes About Friendship

Salt your food with humor,
Pepper it with wit,
And sprinkle over it
The charm of fellowship.

—1929 SCRAPBOOK

Men do not attract that which they want, but that which they are.

—JAMES LANE ALLEN

The man who treasures his friends is usually solid gold himself.

—MARJORIE HOLMES

To communicate with your friend doesn't mean you have to have an answer for their troubles. You just have to be aware of them and share with them and care for them.

—SARA C.

A true friend is one who loves you just as much watching you rise on your way up as when they are catching you on your way down.

—JAMES ROHN

Our opinion of people depends less upon what we see in them than upon what they make us see in ourselves.

—SARA C.

A friend is one who walks in when others walk out.

—WALTER WINCHELL

Three lovely things life gives to me;
Whatever else fate sends,
My heart is filled with gratitude
for trees, and books, and friends.

—ROBERT MCCONN

Helping someone else is the secret of happiness.

—BOOKER T. WASHINGTON

Poems to Send to Friends

NEW FRIENDS

I knew it from the beginning,
I knew it from the start,
You were going to be a friend
That grew inside my heart.
When we first met I was certain,
So now until the end,
It seems I've always known you, and
You've always been my friend.

The day that we met,
I knew we would be
Friends forever—
Yes, that's you and me.

OLD FRIENDS

The fabric of friendship on which we've sewn,
A special bond between us has grown,
A loyalty that only we hold,
Inseparable as friends as we grow old.

FOREVER FRIENDS

If I could be the kind of friend
That you have been to me,
I'd be like you at every turn,
That's how I'd want to be;
I'd follow in your footsteps
And practice all your ways,
And hope that I've been half the friend
You've been throughout my days.

A FRIEND IS SOMEONE SPECIAL

A friend is someone special
Who understands us to a T,
A person who always listens
And doesn't tell us how to be;

A friend is someone precious
Who understands our hopes and fears,
And comes to our rescue daily,
And is treasured through the years.

FOR MY FRIENDS

I am thankful, really thankful,
For all my friends, you see.
My friends are understanding,
They're always there for me.
They sometimes appear in numbers
And unite when I'm in need.
Yes, I am really thankful
To have these friends, indeed!

A FRIEND ON CALL

When something's wrong or something's right,
You're the one I call.
I might feel discombobulated,
Or nothing's wrong at all.
You're always there to listen
When I am out of whack.
I'm lucky to have a friend like you . . .
Who always calls me back!

The ABC's of Friendship

*A*lways be honest.
*B*e there when they need you.
*C*heer them on.
*D*on't look for their faults.
*E*very chance you get, call!
*F*orgive them.
*G*et together often.
*H*ave faith in them.
*I*nclude them.
*J*ust listen.
*K*now their dreams.
*L*ove them unconditionally.
*M*ake them feel special.
*N*ever forget them.
*O*ffer to help.
*P*raise them honestly.
*Q*uietly disagree.
*R*escue them often.
*S*ay you're sorry.
*T*alk frequently.
*U*se good judgment.
*V*ote for them!
*W*ish them good luck!
X-ray yourself first.
*Y*our word counts.
*Z*ip your mouth when told a secret.

Creative Ideas for Celebrating Your Friends

GIVE YOUR FRIEND A PH.D. IN FRIENDSHIP. When my wonderful friend Ava got her Ph.D., a group of her friends gave a dinner in her honor. In gracious acceptance of all this attention, Ava reversed the opportunity and awarded everyone a Ph.D. in Friendship. She created a thoughtful diploma for each of us that addressed how we had helped her reach her goal: from listening to carpooling, our degree of friendship was registered.

The Institute of Friendship
Confers
With Honors and Distinctions
The Degree of Ph.D. in Friendship

to

___

DELIVER DINNER. When you have a friend who's besieged with too much to do, deliver dinner to their door. Simple menus like pasta with tomato sauce and a salad are appreciated. Add a note that says: "You've got too much cooking, and it's not food. I hope this helps you till you get in the mood."

PLAN A FRIEND'S DAY. Choose one day and tell your friend to save it for you, no excuses accepted. Plan a special day doing all of the favorite things you ordinarily do as friends. Include a movie, lunch, a manicure—you name it. The day will be heaven-sent.

STRIKE IT RICH. Send your friend a lottery ticket with a card that says, "As friends go, you're a winner!" or "I hit the jackpot when you became my friend!"

RENT A TAPE. Rent or loan a tape to a friend who needs a break. Choose a classic and deliver it to their door.

INSTANT RELIEF FOR A FRIEND. Rewrap a medicine bottle and fill with M&M's. Retype the label and say: "For instant relief, take one and call me at (list your telephone number)." You could also write: "To relieve pain, take one and call me at ———."

THE GOLDEN ROLODEX. Send your friend a card with your name and number on it for their Rolodex. Write at the top of it: "When you need a friend, call (your telephone number)."

GO GROCERY SHOPPING WITH YOUR FRIEND. Grab the coupons and your friend, and make a weekly chore fun again. You'll discover great new foods and have fun doing it together.

SEND A CARD A DAY. If your friend needs cheering up, send a card a day for a week.

FRIENDS FOREVER. Bring or send your friend a copy of the Broadway musical *Grease*, which features the song "We Go Together." Enclose a card that says those words.

YEARBOOK SURPRISE. Create a "This Is Your Life" for a friend. Secretly borrow and photocopy pages from your friend's high school yearbook. Create a book filled with the person's class photo, the flattering notes accompanying it, and inscriptions from friends; or use the paper to wrap a gift. Include a teacher or two from the past when possible, too. This one will take plotting, but your friend will love every inch of it!

FRIENDS ON THE GO. Pack up a container filled with sugarless gum, candy, and favorite snacks your friend adores. Hide the package in their glove compartment or backseat with a note that says, "In case you need a snack or two, I made this package just for you!"

CREATE A SPECIAL PERSONALIZED RECIPE FOR YOUR FRIEND.

Recipe for a Friendship

1 cup loyalty
2 cups kindness
3 teaspoons forgiveness
5 tablespoons time for each other
4 gallons honesty
1 cup faith

Combine all ingredients with love and affection, and mix carefully. Stir well, and should you notice any lumps or flaws, handle gently and overlook as often as possible. Sweeten generously with a firm belief in each other and keep warm with a caring heart and a watchful eye. Never serve hot or cold, just room temperature. Let stand for a lifetime of special memories.

Add the recipe to a box of sugar and write, "Thank you for sweetening my life with your friendship!"

FOR A FRIEND WHO ALWAYS HAS JUICY NEWS.
Since 1946, Blue Heron has been shipping Florida's finest, juiciest
citrus fruit. Call 1-800-237-3920 and order your friend the gift of
juicy oranges. Prices begin at $12.95 and include shipping, which
only happens from November to May when oranges are in season.
Request a free catalog. Have a note added to your order that says,
"Orange you glad we're friends? I sure am!"

BOOMERANG BROWNIES. Call 1-800-736-4069, Brownies
on Tour, and order the brownies of your dreams. From Black Forest
Brownies to Kitty Hawk Brownies, there's something for everyone.
These handmade, freshly baked brownies arrive quickly and are so
good, you'll want to send them right back to get even with a friend
who has sent them to you.

SHOP TILL YOU DROP. Call 1-800-777-0000 and order
Bloomingdale's by Mail, Ltd., catalog and send it to a friend. They'll
love this tempting presentation for the real shopper at heart. Add a
note that says, "Even if I shopped all day, I'd only find one you!" or
"When I went shopping for a friend, I was lucky to find you!"

MUSIC TO THEIR EARS. The San Francisco Music Box
Company, at 1-800-227-2190, can customize a music box with any
of their songs from their tune list. Send a special friend "That's What
Friends Are For" or "You've Got a Friend." Request their free catalog
and choose the perfect gift that will play on demand anytime your
friend needs inspiration!

SEND A PEN PAL. Since 1950, World Pen Pals has served more than 20,000 young people with international pen pals every year. If you are twelve to twenty years old, write to them at 1694 Como Ave., St. Paul, MN 55108. The cost is $4.50 for one pen pal, $8.50 for two, $12 for four, or $3 per person for a group of six or more. Include your name, address, age, hobbies, languages spoken, the service fee, a list of five countries of interest, and a self-addressed envelope.

9

Words of Appreciation and Gratitude

Those who bring sunshine to the lives of others
cannot keep it from themselves.

—JAMES M. BARRIE

When an adult or a child discovers that their words of gratitude and grateful actions matter, they are bound to use them more often. An appreciative heart is a special one, for it notices the little things in life, the details. Consider someone, for example, who has done something special for you. Have you told them how much it meant to you? Even if it's by telephone, it's never too late to tell someone that something they did matters.

When you express gratitude, you share your innermost appreciation for someone as you mark the moment with this memorable gesture. Often, though, we are so busy we forget to take time to put our thanks into words and actions. Don't miss the chance to express your gratitude; it will lead you to a deeper sense of happiness and connection with others.

When writing a note of appreciation or expressing your gratitude, keep these initials in mind: K.I.S.S., which stand for Keep It Sincere and Specific. Speak from your heart and describe what you are thankful for. Don't just say, "Thank you for your kind deed," tell someone what they did that made you feel special and that you appreciate it! If somebody prepared dinner for you, mention what you ate and how much you enjoyed it. Even if the dinner your friend made wasn't your favorite or you are allergic to tuna casserole, you can still focus on how much time they spent preparing it and what they mean to you as a friend.

Quotes About Appreciation

A kind heart is a fountain of gladness, making everything in its vicinity freshen into smiles.

—WASHINGTON IRVING

One of the most difficult things to ever give away is kindness, for it is usually returned.

—ANONYMOUS

You cannot do a kindness too soon, for you never know how soon it will be too late.

—RALPH WALDO EMERSON

I thank you for your voices, thank you, / Your most sweet voices.

—WILLIAM SHAKESPEARE

What wisdom can you give that is greater than kindness.

—JEAN JACQUES ROUSSEAU

Flattery is from the teeth out. Sincere appreciation is from the heart out.

—DALE CARNEGIE

The most exquisite pleasure is giving pleasure to others.

—JEAN DE LA BRUYÈRE

If you want something done, ask a busy person.

—BENJAMIN FRANKLIN

Blessed is the influence of one true, human soul on another.

—GEORGE ELIOT

Life is mostly froth and bubble;
Two things stand like stone:
Kindness in another's trouble,
Courage in your own.

—ADAM LINDSAY GORDON

Words of Appreciation

I APPRECIATE YOUR GIFT

It's not the gifts that I receive
That end up meaning the most to me;
It's the joy it brings, the special thought,
With which the gift to me was brought.

It's not the gifts that can be bought
That become life's little treasures;
It's gifts that come from the heart,
The ones that can't be measured.
It's gifts of friendship, tried and true,
That become life's gifts of gold;
These gifts of kindness can't be bought
For they're too precious to be sold.

A GIVING HEART

There are rare and special people
Who always give and give;
To them it's nothing special,
It's just how they choose to live.
They never are too busy,
No matter what the task;
They seem to think of everything
Before you even ask.
These people are quite special,
They're rare and kind and few;
I'm thankful, though, that I have found
One of them—that's you!

JUST FOR YOU!

I wrote this poem because I think you're great,
You're someone I appreciate!
I hope you know this through and through—
To thank you once just wouldn't do!

Here's a thank-you note my dad wrote us after a birthday dinner when my mom was out of town:

Dear Robyn, Willy, Justin, and Ali,

Thank you so much for making my birthday truly special. The cards, the gifts, and dinner at my favorite restaurant. And if that wasn't enough—a wonderful birthday cake with candles, wonderful words, and then later at

home—in the kitchen with Doug's method of "no mess serving," paper plates, paper napkins, and when finished—no crumbs—no mess—no kitchen disturbance —clean as a whistle. All of this was truly great.

But the real important happening was all of your caring and love and doing it up so special—I'm truly blessed . . . "My cup runneth over."

ALL MY LOVE AND APPRECIATION,

DAD

MORE NOTES OF GRATITUDE

Dear ——,

For all the marvelous, wonderful, thoughtful, considerate things you do every day . . . thank you!

You gave us a special, memorable night. Thank you for being such a great friend,

LOVE,

Dear Robyn,
Really
Outstanding
Book!
You have
iNspired me.
Your friend, Patrick

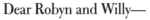

Dear Robyn and Willy—

What have I done to deserve all this lavish attention?!? You really know how to make someone feel special. As if that breathtaking white orchid wasn't enough, I'm serenaded by Frank Sinatra as well. If I'd known turning fifty was so much fun, I'd have done it a long time ago! Thank you, special friends—you're dear to my heart.

FONDLY,
ROSEMARY

Dear ——,

Every birthday is special, but you have made this year a birthday I'll never forget. You will never have to wonder if you know me inside out! How can I ever thank you enough for the fabulous gift? If I had seen the perfume bottle in a store, I would have picked it out myself. You always seem to know what I'll love and treasure. You make such a difference in my life and I feel so lucky to call you my friend.

YOUR BIGGEST FAN,

Making Gratitude Your Business

Regardless of what business you are in, you have probably discovered the importance and value of thanking your clients, your customers, or your employees. Making gratitude your business is a winning way to let others know how much you appreciate them. It's also a more meaningful way to do business.

There are many ways to express your thanks in business, and often it's appropriate to write a letter of appreciation. It's fun to be creative and make your thank-you stand out from the crowd! Here are some ways to say thank you:

WRITE A LETTER OF APPRECIATION TO A CUSTOMER

Dear ——:

I just wanted to stop and write you a letter to thank you for your continued business. Your patronage of our store means so much to all of us, and it's such a pleasure to have you depend on our service and products. We are proud to have you as a customer and look forward to many years of serving your needs. If you ever have a suggestion or way we could serve you better, please do not hesitate to contact me at the store. Thank you for being a valued customer.

SINCERELY,

A LETTER OF APPRECIATION FOR AN EMPLOYEE

Dear ——:

I just wanted to take a moment to tell you what a splendid job you are doing at our office. Everyone who meets you comments on your enthusiasm, and your attention to detail has helped us succeed in many ways. Your positive attitude and keen sensitivity to our customers have made you a valuable member of our team. We are so proud you have joined us!

ALWAYS,

CREATIVE BUSINESS GIFTS. Call 1-800-4-FLOURS (1-800-435-6877)—or in Atlanta 1-404-876-2200—and request a Blooming Cookies catalog, which is filled with delicious long-stemmed cookies and fabulous edible gifts, including blooming bagels and other creative goodies. In response to the growing demand for one-of-a-kind gifts, they have established a Wish Desk and will customize a hand-painted flowerpot with your business name and fill it with blooming cookies. Add a note that says: "Our business is growing thanks to you!"

Dear Teacher

SEND YOUR TEACHER A NOTE OF APPRECIATION

Dear ——,

Henry Brooks Adams once said, "A teacher affects eternity; he can never tell where his influence stops." This quote could well apply to you. You have influenced my life in so many ways. What makes you so remarkable is that while you made a difference in my life, you taught every one of your students with the same enthusiasm, kindness, and dedication.

I will never forget what a difference you made in my life. As I have grown older and hopefully wiser, I have carried many of your valuable lessons along the way.

Thank you for influencing my life,

THE ABC'S OF SCHOOL SUPPLIES. Call 1-800-669-4222 and order the ABC School Supply catalog. It's a fabulous teacher resource book filled with great items that every teacher needs. Send the catalog with a note of thanks: "Thank you for teaching me the ABC's. Enjoy this catalog for you from me!"

Words of Thanks to Choose and Use

Your thoughtfulness always warms my heart.

We have many blessings and are thankful to count you among them.

May the coming year be one of great joy and even more blessings for you and your family.

Thank you again for all of your love and support—it means more than you know.

Thank you for being yourself. That's what being a true friend is all about.

With every good wish I send my eternal thanks.

Your good deeds will never be forgotten.

Clever Ways to Express Your Appreciation

Creative Gifts and Words of Appreciation to Go with Them

Popcorn: Thank you for popping into our lives.

Hammer: Thanks—you knocked us out!

Soap: You lathered us with kindness!

Flowers: We're blooming with appreciation.

Pretzels or anything crunchy: Thanks for helping us in a crunch!

A box of chocolates: Life's a box of chocolates, thanks to you!

Taffy or anything sticky: Thank you for sticking with us!

A check: Fill it in with one million thank-yous!

Sugar-free foods: Thank you to the sweetest person we know!

Picture frame: Thank you for a picture-perfect weekend!

Baseball: Thanks . . . we had a ball!

Dinosaurs of any kind: My thank-you is prehistoric, forgive me!

Puzzle: Our appreciation is endless, just like this puzzle!

Socks, a wool scarf, or anything warm: Your generosity warmed our hearts! Hope this gift does the same for you!

Angel: Here's a heavenly thank-you!

More Gifts to Express Your Appreciation

SEND THE LATEST AND GREATEST CATALOG GUIDE. Send for the Great Catalog Guide and you'll find more than 350 fabulous catalogs with seventy product categories in the Direct Marketing Association's latest edition. Whoever receives this guide will appreciate you all year long! Add a note that says, "When it comes to special people, you're cataloged for life!" Send your name and address with a $3 check or money order to Great Catalog Guide, Consumer Services Dept., Direct Marketing Association, 1111 19th St. NW, Ste. 1100, Washington, DC 20036-3603.

GET READY TO SAY THANK YOU! Call 1-800-643-0042 and order from Current, Inc., a free catalog filled with stationery and cards in appealing designs, with a variety of motifs. There is something for everyone, and personalized stationery makes a great gift! All-occasion and holiday cards are available as well as personalized notes, gift wrapping paper, organizers, and much more. Stock up on an assortment of these and you'll be ready to write.

ADD YOUR PERSONAL TOUCH. Call Personal Creations at 1-800-264-6626 and order a free catalog with an outstanding selection of personalized gifts. Want to send a clever thank-you? Choose a gift from any of these charming items and have it personalized. The recipient will think it's the most original thank-you they ever received!

THANK YOU FOR SPICING UP OUR STAY. Want to thank someone for their wonderful hospitality? Call 1-800-227-4530 and order a free catalog from San Francisco Herb Company. They specialize in herbs and spices, certain to add some spice to your hosts' lives.

GOING WILD OVER SOMETHING? Pack up a basket of wildflower seeds and include a note: "I'm wild about your gift! Thank you!" or "We went wild over your gift!"

INCREDIBLE EDIBLE THANK-YOU. Call Ace Specialty Foods at 1-800-323-9754 and order a chocolate telegram. It's a personalized box of chocolates with sixty pieces of candy and your message printed in chocolate and packaged as a gift. You have up to sixty

spaces available for your message, with twelve letters across and five down. Design a message such as:

To the
Sweetest
Friends
On Earth.
Love, Robyn

HOLY COW! THANK YOU! If someone has "moooved" you in a special way, find a greeting card with a cow on it or purchase a plastic cow and let them know!

THANK SOMEONE FOR EXTENDING THEMSELF. If someone helps you in a pinch, wrap up an extension cord and send it with a note that reads, "Thank you for extending yourself!"

THANKS FOR STICKING WITH ME. Put together an assortment of colorful stickers and self-sticking notes and say thank you to someone who has stuck by you!

MARK THE OCCASION WITH A THANK-YOU. Mark a special occasion with a beautiful bookmark. You can't go wrong with this one, and it'll save those special books from any dog-eared pages.

THANKS FOR ALL YOUR TIME. Send a clock with a note that says thank you to someone special who has given you their time!

THANKS TO A LIVING DOLL. Send a doll with a special note that thanks someone for being an absolute doll!

OUR HATS ARE OFF TO YOU. Fill a cardboard hat from a party supply store with candy and add this note: "Our hats are off to you!"

TURN ON THE CHARM. Send a light bulb with a thank-you to someone who has lightened your load!

A SWEET REMEMBRANCE. Call 1-800-9-GODIVA and send chocolate from one of the country's leading chocolatiers. Send the sweetest thank-you on earth!

STUCK ON SOMEONE? Send a jar of peanut butter and jelly in a basket with a note that says, "Thank you for spreading your kindness!"

SEND A GOURMET THANK-YOU. Call Rowena's at 1-800-627-8699 and order Rowena's free catalog filled with gourmet foods. From almond pound cake to chocolate sauces and carrot jams, this company specializes in sending wonderful delicacies. Be sure to ask about their Cake-of-the-Month Club for someone who really takes the cake.

THINK SOMEONE'S DANDY? Call 1-800-872-6879 and order the Missouri Dandy Pantry catalog filled with nuts, fudge, candy, and delectable gifts guaranteed to make a dandy impression.

SEND A GOURMET THANK-YOU. Order the Pfaelzer Brothers catalog by calling 1-800-621-0226 and order steaks, pasta, cakes, and even low-fat goodies. This company has made special occasions unforgettable since 1923 and has a fabulous selection of gourmet foods.

GREETINGS IN CHOCOLATE. Order the Hershey's Gift Catalog at 1-800-4-KISSES! This catalog lists a host of creative and innovative products created by Hershey's. With anything from a three-pound personalized milk chocolate cake to chocolate greeting cards, let a sweet friend know they are really appreciated.

Recommended Books with Words That Matter

One of the greatest gifts or acts of kindness is to give someone a book that you love and believe might be meaningful to them. Here are some suggestions, with words to add in a card or note:

All I Ever Really Needed to Know I Learned in Kindergarten, by Robert Fulghum; Villard Books, 1986, 1988.
Words to add: *All I ever really needed to learn, I learned from you!*

The Book of Virtues: A Treasury of Great Moral Stories, edited, with commentary, by William J. Bennett; Simon & Schuster, 1993.
Words to add: *To someone of great virtue. . . . Enjoy this book!*

The Bride Did What? Etiquette for the Wedding Impaired, by Martha A. Woodham; Longstreet Press, 1995.
Words to add: *Here comes the perfect bride! You, of course.*

Chicken Soup for the Soul: 101 Stories to Open the Heart and Rekindle the Spirit, by Jack Canfield and Mark Victor Hansen; Health Communications, 1993.
Words to add: *Here's some chicken soup for your soul. . . . May your bowl runneth over!*

A Gift from the Sea, by Anne Morrow Lindbergh; Pantheon Books, 1991.
Words to add: *Wishing you sand castles of happiness and gifts from the sea.*

Good Behavior: Over 1,200 Sensible Solutions to Your Child's Problems, from Birth to Age Twelve, by Drs. Stephen and Marianne Garber and Robyn Freedman Spizman; Villard Books, 1987.
Words to add: *May all your problems be "little ones."*

A Hero in Every Heart: Champions from All Walks of Life Share Powerful Messages to Inspire the Hero in Each of Us, by H. Jackson Brown, Jr., and Robyn Freedman Spizman; Thomas Nelson Publishers, 1996.
Words to add: *To a Hero in My Heart.*

Life's Little Instruction Book, by H. Jackson Brown, Jr.; Rutledge Hill Press, vols. 1–3, 1991–95.
Words to add: *Follow these instructions for a happy life! You deserve it!*

Little Things Long Remembered: Making Your Children Feel Special Every Day, by Susan Newman; Crown Publishers, 1993.
Words to add: *For you my heart will always boast;*
Our time together matters most.

The Thank You Book: Hundreds of Clever, Meaningful, and Purposeful Ways to Say Thank You, by Robyn Freedman Spizman; Longstreet Press, 1994.
Words to add: *A million thanks for one in a million!*

The Wholesale by Mail Catalog: How Consumers Can Shop By Mail, Phone or Online Service; HarperPerennial, 1996 (updated yearly).
Words to add: *Shop 'til you drop and enjoy this book!*

Words That Every Child Must Hear, by Cynthia Good; Longstreet Press, 1994.
Words to add: *No matter where you may go*
And wherever you may be,
These words are from my heart,
With love to you from me.

Acknowledgments

My appreciation goes to you, the reader, as you mark the moment with an act of kindness that will matter most to someone else. My endless affection goes to my wonderful husband, Willy, who supports my hopelessly addictive love of writing, and to our children, Justin and Ali, who provide my daily inspiration and keep me in tune with the little things that matter most. To my dedicated parents, Phyllis and Jack Freedman, whom I love beyond words, to my beloved grandmother, Pauline Blonder, and Aunt Frances Ritchkin for cheering me on, and to Bettye Storne, who joyfully helps me in everything I do.

My appreciation also goes to my literary agent, Meredith Bernstein, for her persistence and patience with my endless ideas, to my wonderful editor, Sharon Squibb, for her encouragement and belief in me, and to H. Jackson Brown, Jr., my friend and mentor, whose little instructions have mattered most.

A special thanks to Lt. Col. McDonald Valentine for his command of quotes, and to the following, who have offered me assistance in immeasurable ways: Drs. Stephen and Marianne Garber, Genie and Doug Freedman, Lois and Jerry Blonder, Ramona and Ely Freedman, Gus Spizman, the late Regina Spizman, Dr. Sam Spizman, Marla and Mark Shavin, Janet Glass, Steve Aveson, Jill Becker, Donna Lowry, Debbie Schechter, Tracy Green, Gail Heyman, Shelley Carey, Deedee Chereton, Francis Klein, Joey Myska, Leslie Isenberg, Joey Reiman, Cynthia Good, Deborah Reeves-Brannon, Ann Battles, Lynn Stallings, Betty Sunshine, Ava Wilensky, Lorie Lewis, Patty Brown, Rosemary Brown, Carla Lovell, Sadie Sacks, Marilyn

Shubin, Wendy Bowman-Littler, Joseph Atchison, Patty Brown, Martha Woodham, Pat Brannon, Jack Morton, Marci Spatz, Bettye Dickson, John McElfrish, Stephanie Pearlmutter, Profiles in History, Joseph M. Maddalena, Lorna Hart, Lori Simon, Dr. Jim Braude, Cheryl Isaacs, Donna Weinstock, Norma Gordon, JacLynn Morris, Mary Billingsley, Faye Edmundson, Patrick Pirkey, Sonia Kuniansky, Brenda Smith, Harvey Rubin, Sean Hepburn Ferrer, and Lara Webb.

Please Note: Every effort was given to acknowledge the accurate sources of all information in this book. Any omissions or errors will be gratefully corrected in a future printing. At the time of publication, every effort was made to ensure the text's accuracy.